WORLD BOOK'S

YOUNG SCIENTIST

WORLD BOOK'S

YOUNG SCIENTIST

• **LIGHT AND ELECTRICITY**
• **MAGNETIC POWER**

4

World Book, Inc.
a Scott Fetzer company
Chicago

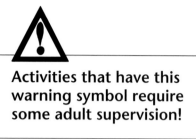

Activities that have this warning symbol require some adult supervision!

The quest to explore the known world and to describe its creation and subsequent development is nearly as old as mankind. In the Western world, the best-known creation story comes from the book of Genesis. It tells how God created Earth and all living things. Modern religious thinkers interpret the Biblical story of creation in various ways. Some believe that creation occurred exactly as Genesis describes it. Others think that God's method of creation is revealed through scientific investigation. *Young Scientist* presents an exciting picture of what scientists have learned about life and the universe.

World Book, Inc.
233 N. Michigan Avenue
Chicago, IL 60601

For information on other World Book products, call 1-800-WORLDBK (967-5325), or visit us at our Web site at http://www.worldbook.com

© 1997, 1995, 1991, 1990 World Book, Inc.

ISBN: 0-7166-2754-X (volume IV)
ISBN: 0-7166-2797-3 (set)

Library of Congress Catalog Card No. 00-107193

Printed in the United States of America

1 2 3 4 5 6 7 06 05 04 03 02 01 00

Contents

Light and electricity

LIGHT AND ELECTRICITY

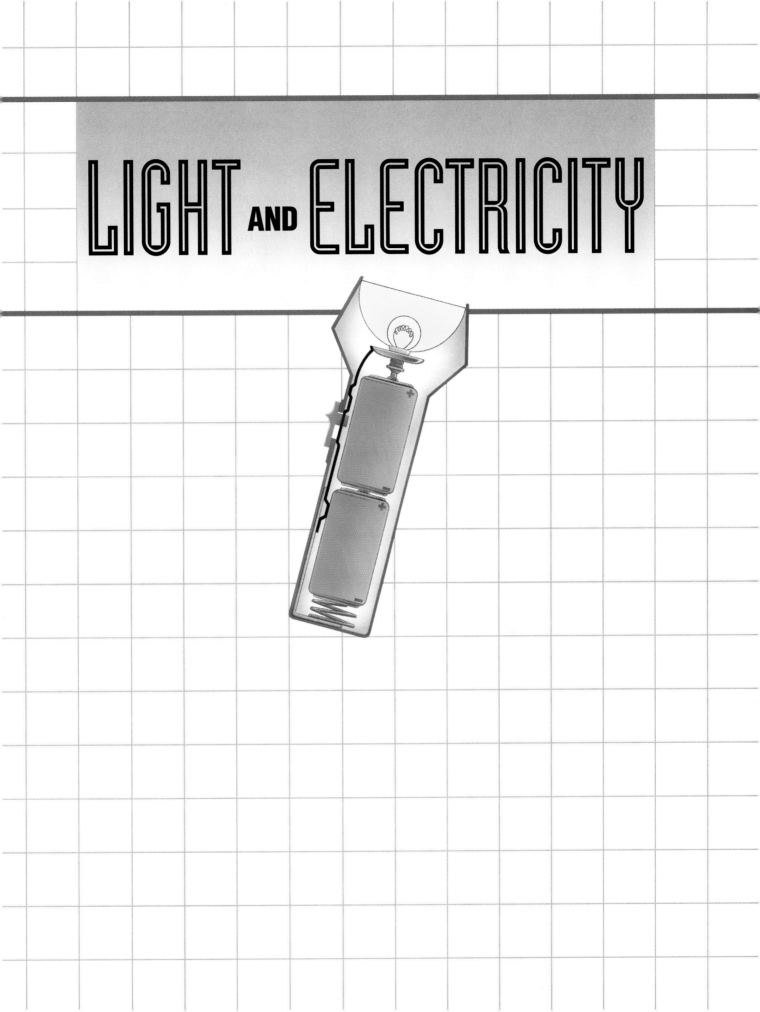

Light from the sun is the most important source of natural light. During daylight, the sun's rays heat and light up Earth.

Where does light come from?

Shut your eyes tight—all you can see is darkness. Now open your eyes again. If it is daytime, you will see that light is all around you.

Natural light

Anything that gives off a light that we can see is called a **light source**. The light sources that are not created by people are called **natural** light sources. They include the sun and the stars. During the day, the rays of the sun light up Earth. At night, if there are no clouds, you can see the stars twinkling in the sky.

There are other sources of natural light, too. In some parts of the world, you can find insects called fireflies. They give off a pale, greenish-yellow light that flashes or glows in the dark. Deep down in the sea, some fish are able to produce flashes of light in the darkness. And if you live in the extreme northern or southern regions of the world, you can often see the **aurora**, a dazzling display of colored lights that flicker in the sky at night.

Artificial light

There are also many light sources that don't occur naturally but are created by people. These are called **artificial** sources of light. Electric lights, oil lamps, and even candles are all artificial light sources. You can find your way in the dark by using a flashlight powered by batteries. Television and movies are made by using light. And city streets are often full of artificial lights—vehicle headlights, brightly colored advertisements, street lights, and neon lights.

Light does more than just enable us to see. We use beams of light to cut metals into complicated shapes, or to perform delicate surgical operations. Light even helps us stay healthy. When sunlight shines on our skin, our body makes a vitamin called vitamin D, which helps our teeth and bones to grow healthy.

In this photograph, light travels through threads of glass called optical fibers. Each fiber is only 1/25 inch (1 millimeter) thick.

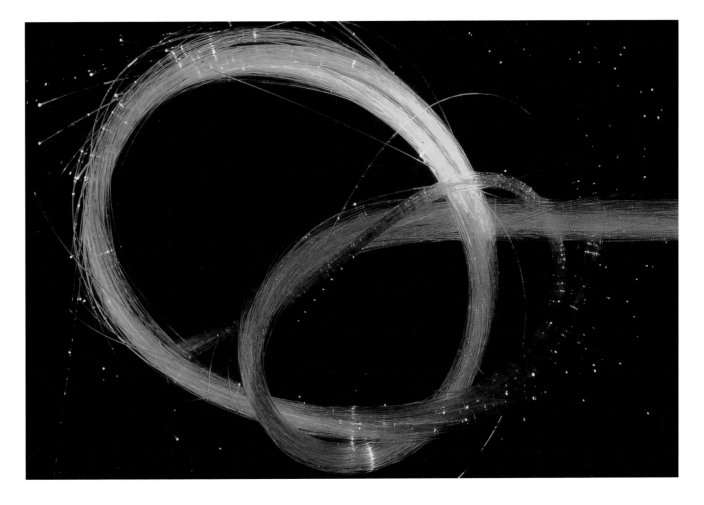

A gas stove burns gas that produces a blue flame. You can make the flame bigger by turning the knob and increasing the flow of gas.

The burning wax of a candle gives off a lot of heat.

A fluorescent light shines with a brilliant white light. Fluorescent bulbs use less electricity than ordinary light bulbs to give the same amount of light.

Light and heat

Take a look around the room you're in. How many different things can you see that are able to give off, or **emit**, light? You could do a survey of the light sources in your home. Make a list of the light sources in each room. After each item on your list, write the color of the light and whether it gives off heat as well.

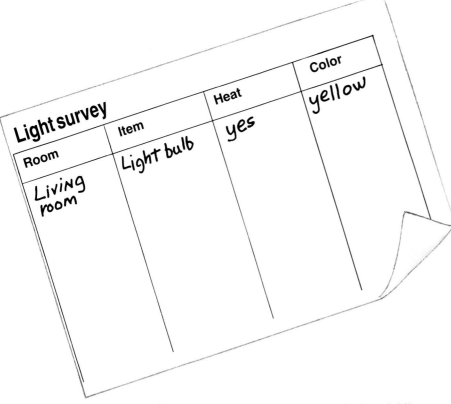

Light survey			
Room	Item	Heat	Color
Living room	Light bulb	yes	yellow

Find out more by looking at pages **24–25**

You'll probably find a lot of different objects that emit light at home. Do most of these give off heat?

Color

You will see that the items on your list don't all emit light of the same color. The flame of a gas stove is blue, and the light from a flashlight is yellowish-white. A flashlight bulb shines a dull orange as the batteries run down.

Heat ⚠️

Place your hand about 2 inches (5 centimeters) away from an electric light bulb, being very careful not to touch the bulb! Can you feel the heat that the bulb gives off? The bulb is using electricity, or electrical energy, to produce both light and heat. The light from the bulb is being used, but the heat is not used—it is wasted energy.

A special kind of light called a **fluorescent light** can be used to change more of the electrical energy into light and less into heat. Try holding your hand close to a fluorescent light. Does it feel as hot as the light bulb?

Find out more by looking at pages **28–29**

How does light travel?

What is light? We can say that light is like a series of waves. Light travels from its source equally in every direction. Light waves from the sun must travel millions of miles before they reach Earth. By the time they reach Earth, each wave is so slightly curved that it is almost a straight line. Each wave always travels like this unless it meets something that makes it change direction. One way that light changes direction is by **reflection.**

Reflection

A beam of light travels through space in a straight line unless something makes it bend. If you shine a flashlight at a mirror, you can see how the light is reflected off the mirror's flat surface and changes direction.

This thin beam of strong light travels in a straight line until it hits the hand. This light is reflected off the hand and then travels in a different direction.

You will need:

a pin

a piece of thick, black paper

a flashlight

some adhesive tape

Light travels in straight lines

You can show how light travels in straight lines, using a flashlight. It is best to do this experiment at night.

1. With the pin, make a hole in the center of the black paper.

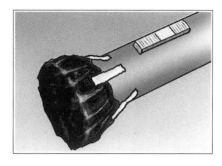

2. Fasten the paper over the head of the flashlight with adhesive tape.

3. Switch off all the lights and switch on the flashlight. Point the flashlight toward a wall. It will light up only a very small area.

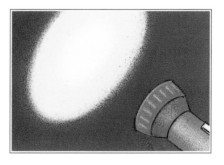

4. Tear off the paper, and point the flashlight toward the wall again. The flashlight will now light up a much bigger area.

If rays of light didn't travel in straight lines, the light coming out through the hole would spread out and light up much more of the room. Instead, the light from the pinhole lights up only a small area.

Reflecting light

Stand behind a doorway and hold up a mirror to see what is happening in the next room. Light rays reflected from objects in the next room are reflected again by the mirror into your eyes.

This and other diagrams in this book show light rays as straight lines. The arrows indicate the direction in which the light travels.

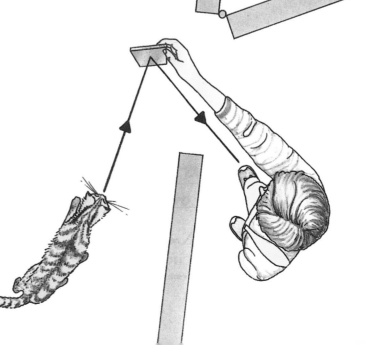

Find out more by looking at pages **16–17**

Colors and white light

Next time you see a rainbow in the sky, look carefully at its colors. On the outside of the rainbow you will see red, and on the inside you will see blue or violet. Sometimes, you can see a faint second rainbow above the first one, with the colors in the opposite order.

How do rainbows form?

Sunlight appears to have no colors. We call it **white light**, but it is really made up of different colors. When you see a rainbow, you see white light that has traveled through millions of falling raindrops.

White light is a mixture of all the colors of the rainbow—red, orange, yellow, green, blue, violet, and all the colors in between. When white light meets a drop of rain, it changes direction. This change of direction is called **refraction**. Some colors in the light change direction more than others, and so the white light separates into its different colors.

A beam of light bends as it passes through a glass prism. The prism splits the light into the colors of the rainbow.

Make a rainbow!

You can make your own rainbow using a specially shaped piece of solid glass called a **prism**. There's a prism in the photograph on the opposite page. White light shines onto one side of the prism and bends as it travels through the glass. When it comes out at the other side, the light has been refracted and separated into its different colors.

On a sunny day, you can also make a rainbow using a mirror.

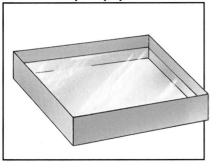 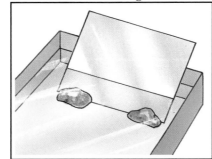

1. Fill the tray with water to a depth of about 1 inch (2.5 centimeters). Place the tray by a window. Draw the curtains so that only a narrow shaft of sunlight enters the room.

2. Rest the mirror in the water at an angle, using modeling clay to make it stand up. Move the tray until the sunlight falls directly on the mirror.

You will need:

water

modeling clay

a piece of white cardboard or thick paper

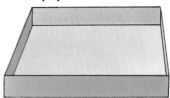

a shallow tray

a small mirror

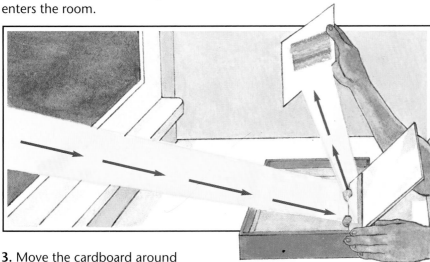

3. Move the cardboard around between the tray and the window until you see a rainbow appear on it. You may have to move the mirror to get this just right.

Look around your house for ornaments made of solid glass. Can you see the different colors of the rainbow when you hold one of the ornaments in the sunlight? Be very careful, as the ornament may be fragile.

Find out more by looking
at pages **14–15**
      18–19
      20–21

Colors and wavelength

Try to think of light as something that travels like **waves.**
White light can be split up into different colors because each
color is made up of waves of a particular length. The distance
between the top of one wave and the top of the next wave
is called the **wavelength,** and each color has its own
wavelength. The color violet has the shortest wavelength.
Red has the longest wavelength.

The primary colors of light

The colors of the rainbow include red, orange, yellow, green,
blue, and violet. But these are not the only colors in the
rainbow. If you look carefully at a rainbow, you can see that
there are colors in between these. This is true for all the other
main colors as well. The whole range of these colors is called
the **spectrum.**

Three of the colors in the spectrum—red, green, and blue—
can be combined in nearly equal amounts to make white
light. That is why they are called the **primary colors of light.**
By using two or three of these colors in the right amounts,
you can make any other color of light in the spectrum.

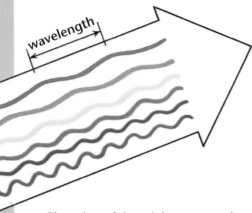

*The colors of the rainbow are made
up of waves. Each color has its own
wavelength.*

*A rainbow is formed in the sky when
sunlight falls on drops of rain, often at
the end of a summer thunderstorm.*

When red and green lights are mixed, the result is yellow light. A mixture of blue and green light forms blue-green light, and blue and red lights form magenta light. Combining all three primary colors in light in the proper proportions results in white light.

Find out more by looking
at pages **12–13**
            14–15
            16–17

18

Colored objects

When you look around your home, you will see lots of different colors. Most people like to have plenty of color in their home. Colors can make a room look bright and cheerful.

How do we see these different colors? White light, such as sunlight, is a mixture of all the colors of the rainbow. When sunlight falls onto a white surface, we see white because all the colors are **reflected** back at us. A surface which reflects no color at all looks black. This is because all the colors have been taken in, or **absorbed**, by the surface.

How do you change a color?

When sunlight falls on a sunflower, the petals absorb all the colors except yellow. When you look at a sunflower, you see it as yellow because yellow is the color most strongly reflected by the sunflower.

How can you change the color of a sunflower without actually painting it? You can shine a colored light onto it. If you shine blue light onto a sunflower, the flower will look almost black. This is because the blue light is absorbed by the flower, and not reflected by it. The sunflower cannot reflect yellow because there is no yellow in the light. So the blue light appears to take away the sunflower's yellow color.

These sunflowers are reflecting yellow light. All the other colors in the spectrum have been absorbed by the petals.

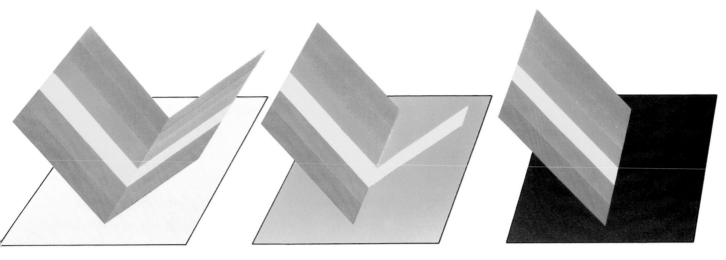

When white light shines on a white surface, all the colors in the spectrum are reflected.

Here, all the colors except yellow have been absorbed by the yellow surface.

A surface that appears to be black reflects no light at all. All the colors have been absorbed by this surface.

You will need:

several sheets of translucent colored plastic or paper

adhesive tape

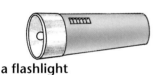

a flashlight

different colored objects

Changing colors

You can do some interesting experiments using a flashlight and colored plastic. The plastic must allow colored light to shine through it. We call such plastic **translucent** plastic.

1. Tape a piece of colored plastic across the front of the flashlight.

2. Shine the flashlight onto each colored object in turn. Make a note of the change in color. Write down, for example, "blue light makes yellow look black." Try using all the colored plastics on each object.

20

Find out more by looking at pages **16–17**
22–23

The invisible spectrum

Light is a type of energy that can travel through space. The energy of light is called **radiant energy.** There are many different kinds of radiant energy. But we can see only a tiny part of the radiant energy that comes from the sun. This tiny part is called the **visible spectrum.** The radiant energy that we cannot see is called the **invisible spectrum.**

Radiant energy is made up of waves of energy called **electromagnetic waves.** Light is one kind of electromagnetic wave. Radio waves, microwaves, ultraviolet rays, and infrared rays are other kinds of electromagnetic waves. The waves together form the **electromagnetic spectrum.** This is a combination of the visible spectrum and the invisible spectrum.

Ultraviolet rays

The sun is the most important natural source of ultraviolet rays. Most of the ultraviolet rays that are emitted by the sun never reach Earth's surface at all. Ultraviolet is very powerful and can be harmful to living things.

If a lot more of the sun's ultraviolet rays passed through Earth's atmosphere, they would probably destroy most plant and animal life on Earth. Fortunately, there is a layer of a gas called **ozone** high up in the atmosphere. Ozone prevents most of the ultraviolet rays from reaching us on Earth.

Earth is surrounded by a protective layer of gas, called ozone. The ozone layer stops most of the harmful ultraviolet rays from reaching Earth's surface.

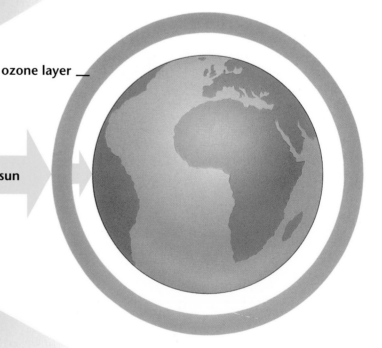

ozone layer __

ultraviolet rays from the sun

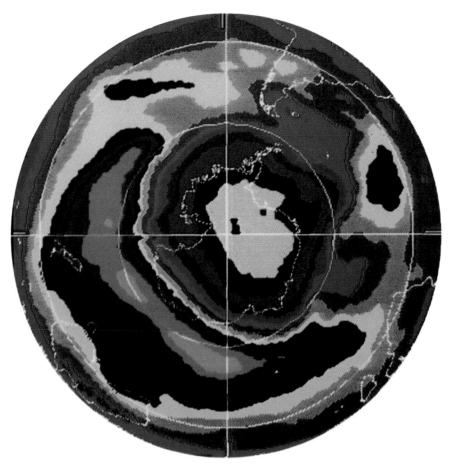

Most of the ultraviolet rays from the sun are absorbed by the ozone layer that surrounds Earth. In this satellite photograph, low concentrations of ozone are shown in purple. High ozone concentrations are in orange and red. Can you see the hole in the ozone layer above the continent of Antarctica?

Helpful and harmful effects

We may not be able to see ultraviolet rays, but they have an important effect on our lives. We all need some ultraviolet light to shine on our skins because it helps our bodies make vitamin D. This vitamin is needed for bones and teeth to grow strong and healthy.

But ultraviolet rays can be harmful as well as helpful. Too much exposure to ultraviolet rays can cause sunburn and skin cancer.

Our skin gives us some protection from ultraviolet rays by producing a substance called **melanin.** If exposed to strong sunlight, the skin produces more melanin and becomes darker. Melanin helps prevent sunburn caused by ultraviolet rays. But if the skin cannot produce enough melanin, it becomes sunburned. Lotions that contain substances that block ultraviolet rays help prevent sunburn and other damage to the skin. But the best way we can protect ourselves from the effects of ultraviolet rays is to avoid spending too much time in the sun.

 To avoid the dangers of ultraviolet rays, don't expose your skin to the sun for long periods. Be sure to use skin lotions that contain sunscreens.

This scientist is carrying out an experiment under ultraviolet light. She wears protective glasses to shield her eyes from the ultraviolet light. Ultraviolet rays are invisible. They lie just beyond the violet end of the spectrum. In this experiment, the source of ultraviolet rays has also produced some blue and violet light.

Find out more by looking at pages **20–21**

Infrared rays

We cannot see **infrared rays**, but we can feel them as heat. It is the infrared rays in sunlight that help to make us feel warm when we stand in the sunshine. Anything that is warm gives out infrared rays. Some animals, such as rattlesnakes, can detect infrared rays given off by other living things. This helps them to catch their prey.

Some burglar alarms work by detecting the infrared heat given off by burglars when they have broken into a building. These alarms have to be carefully adjusted so that they aren't set off by the infrared heat from smaller animals, such as cats! Infrared remote control is used to operate TV sets and videocassette recorders (VCR's).

Can you figure out which are the houses in this infrared aerial photograph of a small town? The trees, grass, and other plants outside the town show up as red.

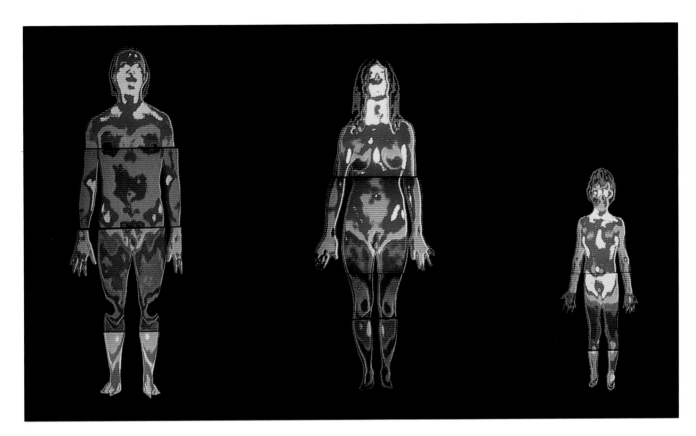

These thermograms show up body temperatures very clearly. The hottest parts look white. The next hottest are red, then orange, green, and blue down to the coolest areas, which are purple.

Using infrared rays

Photographs can be taken in complete darkness by using **infrared film**, which is sensitive to infrared heat rays. This type of film takes a "heat picture" instead of a light picture. The photograph is then printed in visible colors so that we can see what is in the picture.

Infrared rays are used in medicine. Special infrared photographs of the body, called **thermograms**, can show up diseased parts because they radiate more heat than healthy parts. Infrared rays are also used to treat muscle pain.

A heat picture of the land taken from the air shows different patches of color. These colors are not the land's real colors. Instead, they represent different amounts of infrared heat radiating from the ground. The picture can also reveal diseased crops. Dead or dying plants give off fewer infrared rays than living plants, and this shows up as a particular color in the photograph.

24

Find out more by looking
at pages **16–17**
        20–21
        22–23

Atoms and light

Scientists have found two main ways of making light. One way is to heat something until it glows, like the coiled wire inside an electric light bulb. The other way is to pass an electric current through a gas, as in a fluorescent tube or bulb. These lamps have a glass tube filled with a fluorescent gas, such as argon. In both cases, light comes from tiny particles of matter called **atoms.** How does this happen?

Atoms and electrons

Matter, whether it is solid, liquid, or gas, is made of atoms. Atoms are so small that we cannot see them. Even the smallest speck you can see under a simple microscope contains 10 billion atoms! Each atom has a central part called a **nucleus.** Tiny particles called **electrons** whirl around this nucleus. The energy of an atom's electrons provides the energy for light.

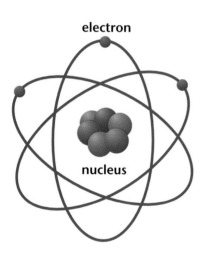

An atom is made of a central part, called the nucleus, and tiny particles called electrons. These electrons whirl around the outside of the nucleus.

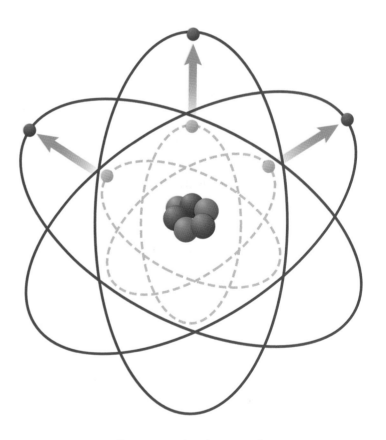

Atoms can absorb energy from outside themselves and become excited. Their electrons then move farther away from the nucleus.

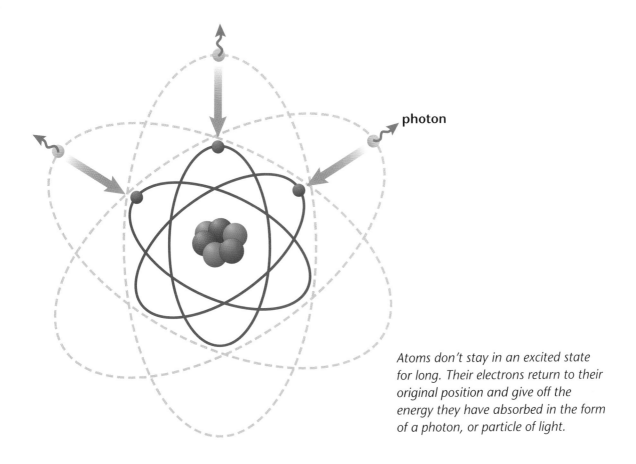

photon

Atoms don't stay in an excited state for long. Their electrons return to their original position and give off the energy they have absorbed in the form of a photon, or particle of light.

Packets of light

When a substance is heated, or electricity is passed through it, its atoms absorb energy. Scientists say that the atoms are **excited.** As each atom becomes more excited, one or more of its electrons can move farther away from its nucleus.

But atoms don't exist in an excited state for long. When electrons return to their former level of energy, they move back closer to the nucleus. They give off the energy they have absorbed. This is usually given off in packets or particles of light energy, which scientists call **photons.** Light is made up of streams of photons.

Emitting white light

When electrons emit light energy, they give off photons with different amounts of energy. These photons make up light of different colors. The photons of red light at one end of the spectrum are less energetic than the photons of violet light at the other end. When photons of these different colors mix together, they produce white light.

What is refraction?

When light passes from one substance to another, it may also change direction. When light rays pass from air to water or from water to air, they bend as they pass through the surface of the water. This bending is called **refraction.**

You will need:

a glass

water

a pencil

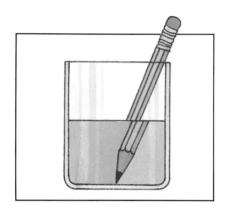

1. Fill the glass halfway with water. Put a pencil in the glass and lean it against the side.

Can you bend a pencil?

Can you bend a pencil without breaking it? You can make a pencil look as if it has been bent, by putting it in water.

2. Look at the water from the side. The pencil will look bent.

3. Now take the pencil out of the water. Nothing has happened to it after all!

Why did the pencil look bent when it was in the water? Light rays speed up as they leave the water and change direction before reaching your eyes. This makes the pencil look bent, and the point of the pencil appears to be halfway up the glass!

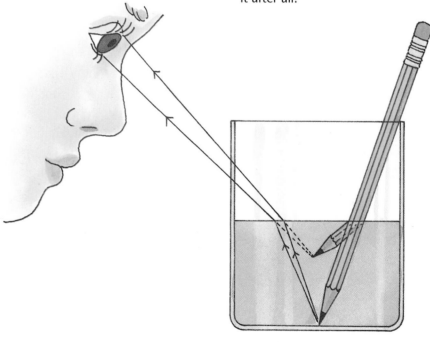

The angle of refraction

Light rays pass through other substances, besides air and water. They travel at different speeds in these substances. As rays pass out of one substance and into another, they are refracted.

The amount that light is refracted depends on two things. The first is the color of the light. Red light bends less than other colors, and violet light bends more. The second is the angle at which the light reaches the surface of the second substance. This is called the **angle of incidence.**

The angle at which the light leaves the surface of the second substance is called the **angle of refraction.** Try your experiment again, looking at the pencil from a number of different angles. You will see that the pencil seems to bend more at some viewing angles than at others.

Find out more by looking at pages **12–13**
14–15

What is a mirage?

The photograph shows a mirage in the desert in Tunisia. The heat makes light rays refract as they pass from cool air down to the hot air near the ground. This makes you think there is a cloud above the sand, but it's not really there. It's a **mirage!** The man in the diagram thinks that he can see a cloud. But rays from the cloud above are creating a mirage on the sand in front of him.

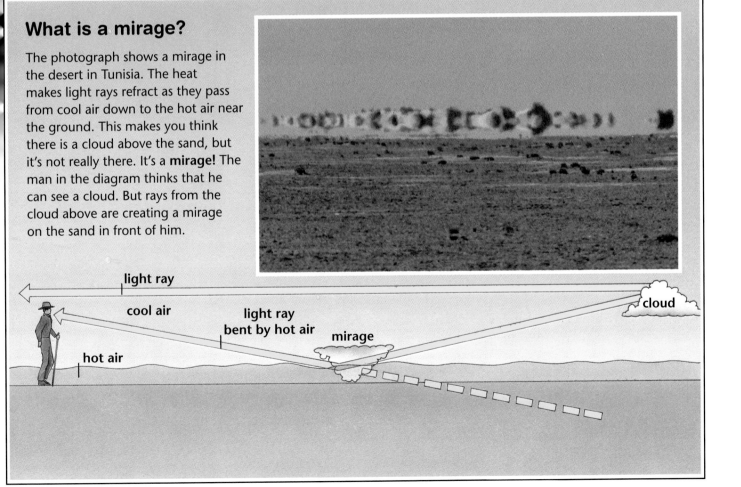

light ray

cool air

light ray
bent by hot air

mirage

cloud

hot air

A perfect mirror image of the Taj Mahal in India is seen in the water.

Mirrors and reflection

Stand in front of a mirror. What do you see? There seems to be a face just like yours behind the mirror. You are looking at a reflection of your face.

You can see things around you because light is reflected from them and then enters your eyes. Mirrors are very good at reflecting light. The light that moves from your face towards the mirror is reflected back by the mirror and enters your eyes. There seems to be another you behind the mirror because the light has come back to its source—you.

Mirrors are made from a sheet of glass with a shiny metal coating on the back. It is this layer of metal that reflects the light. Most mirrors are flat, so the reflection, or **image**, of an object looks the same size and shape as the object itself. This type of mirror is called a **plane mirror**.

Images at an angle

When you look in a mirror that is set at an angle, you don't always see yourself. You might see a different image. This is because the direction in which the light travels is changed by the mirror. One instrument that uses mirrors to help you see around corners is a **periscope**. A simple periscope consists of a long tube with a reflecting mirror set at an angle at each end. Periscopes are used in submarines. Scientists also use periscopes to watch dangerous chemical reactions in laboratories.

Find out more by looking at pages **12–13**

Make a periscope

You can make a simple periscope for yourself.

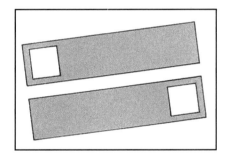

1. Cut a square 2 inches (5 cm) square, about 1/2 inch (1.25 cm) from one end of each of two cardboard strips.

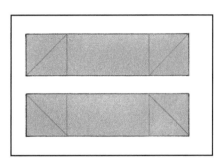

2. Draw a straight line 3 inches (7.5 cm) from each end of the other strips of cardboard. Then draw diagonal lines as shown.

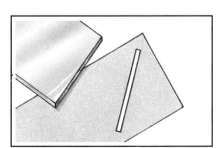

3. Cut a slot 3 inches (7.5 cm) long along each diagonal line. The slot must be big enough for a mirror to fit into it.

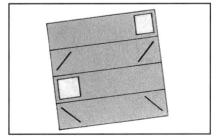

4. On a flat surface, lay out the four pieces of cardboard as shown. Tape them together.

5. Tape together the two long sides. Fold the assembled boards to make a box.

You will need:

four strips of cardboard, **12 in. (30 cm) × 3 in. (7.5 cm)**

scissors

a ruler

a pencil

adhesive tape

two small mirrors, about 3 in. (7.5 cm) square

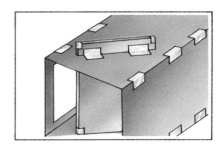

6. Carefully apply tape to the corners of the mirrors so they are not so sharp. Push a mirror through each pair of slots. Make sure the fronts of the mirrors are facing each other. Put some tape along each slot to keep the mirrors from sliding.

7. Now you are ready to look around corners and over heads in a crowd!

Looking through telescopes

Have you ever looked through a telescope? It makes faraway objects seem much nearer. You may even have your own telescope. If so, it probably is a **refracting telescope.**

Refracting telescopes

A refracting telescope has a piece of glass, called a **lens**, at each end of a narrow tube. The large lens at the front of the tube bends, or refracts, the light that enters it. It produces an image at the other end that you can view through a second lens, called the **eyepiece.**

Refracting telescopes are simple, but their strength is limited by the size of the lens inside. The world's largest refracting telescope has a lens that measures about 40 inches (1 meter) across.

To make a huge mirror for a telescope, workers load blocks of glass into a massive mold. A large, rotating oven heats the mold, which melts the glass in the shape required for a telescope mirror.

The Keck telescopes in Hawaii are the world's largest reflecting telescopes.

Reflecting telescopes

Astronomers normally use **reflecting telescopes**. These contain curved mirrors instead of lenses. The mirrors are able to collect more light than the lenses. This is important when astronomers are looking at very distant stars and planets. The Keck I and Keck II telescopes in Hawaii are the world's largest reflecting telescopes. They use large curved mirrors that form a reflecting surface that measures 33 feet (10 meters) across. It's so good at gathering light that you could use it to see a candle flame 15,500 miles (25,000 kilometers) away!

The main mirror in a reflecting telescope is **concave**. This means that its surface is shaped like the inside of a bowl. When the telescope is pointed at an object, light rays from the object are collected and **focused** by the mirror. The rays are then reflected onto one or more other mirrors before being viewed.

Most astronomers use television monitors or computers to view, record, and analyze what is being observed through the telescope.

32

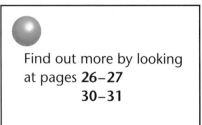

Find out more by looking
at pages **26–27**
30–31

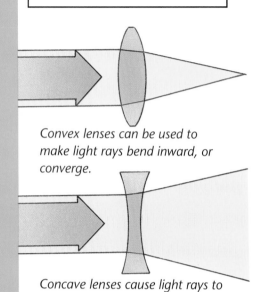

Convex lenses can be used to make light rays bend inward, or converge.

Concave lenses cause light rays to spread out, or diverge.

How do lenses work?

A lens is a piece of transparent material that has at least one curved surface. Lenses refract rays of light to form images of an object. They are usually made of glass or plastic and they are used in cameras, telescopes, and other instruments.

Your eyes have natural lenses. These important parts enable your eyes to form sharp images of near and distant objects.

Convex and concave lenses

Convex lenses are thicker in the middle than at the top and bottom. They can be used to make light rays that pass through them refract, and come closer together, or **converge**. Convex lenses may be used to make things look bigger, or **magnified**.

Concave lenses are thicker at the top and bottom than in the middle. They make light rays spread out, or **diverge**. Objects seen through a concave lens look smaller.

Astronomers use large telescopes with both convex and concave lenses. Eyeglasses made of concave lenses help correct the vision of people with poor distance vision. Eyeglasses made of convex lenses correct vision in people who have trouble seeing objects up close.

You will need:

a piece of cardboard, about
4 in. (10 cm) × 6 in. (15 cm)

scissors

water and milk

modeling clay

a bright flashlight

a glass bottle or jar

How do convex lenses refract light?

You can see how convex lenses refract the light passing through them by doing this experiment.

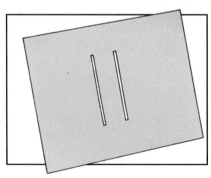

1. Cut a pair of thin slits in the cardboard. Each slit should be 2 inches (5 cm) long. Leave 0.5 inch (1.25 cm) of space between slits.

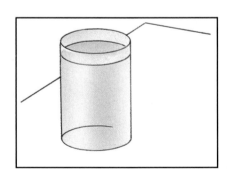

2. Pour some water and a few drops of milk into the bottle or jar, and place it about 6 inches (15 cm) from the edge of a table. Switch on your flashlight, and switch off the lights.

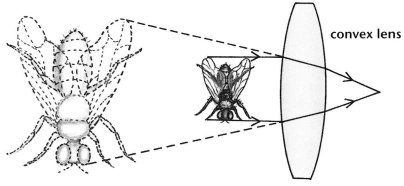

large image of a fly

Convex lens

Look at an object, such as a fly, through a convex lens. The fly will be magnified and appear bigger than it really is.

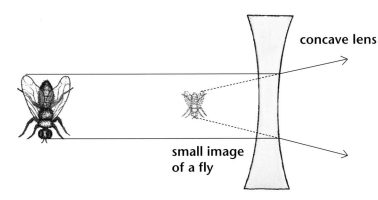

small image of a fly

Concave lens

Look at a fly through a concave lens and it will appear smaller than it really is.

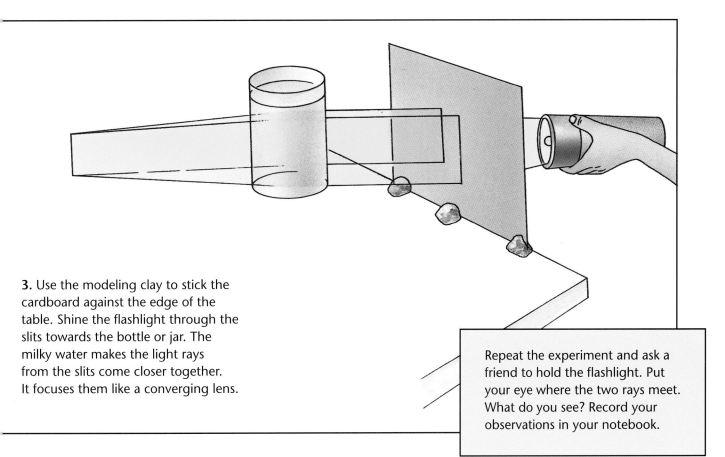

3. Use the modeling clay to stick the cardboard against the edge of the table. Shine the flashlight through the slits towards the bottle or jar. The milky water makes the light rays from the slits come closer together. It focuses them like a converging lens.

Repeat the experiment and ask a friend to hold the flashlight. Put your eye where the two rays meet. What do you see? Record your observations in your notebook.

How do cameras work?

Cameras can be very expensive to buy or they can cost very little. You can even buy a camera that you throw away when you have used up the film! But all film cameras use the same main parts to make pictures. When the camera's shutter opens, light that is reflected off the scene being photographed strikes the lens. The light passes through the lens and makes an image on the film at the back of the camera. Look at the drawing to see the main parts of the camera and how they work together to make pictures.

The **viewfinder** shows you the picture you are about to take with the camera. Some viewfinders allow you to look through them and the camera lens at the same time. Many viewfinders have a mechanism to let you know if there is enough light to take a picture.

The **film** inside the camera is sensitive to light. It is coated with chemicals that change when light shines on them. These chemicals change more quickly on some films than on others.

If you are taking photographs on a cloudy day or indoors, you use a "fast" film, which is very sensitive to light. On a bright, sunny day, you use a "slow" film.

The inside lining of the **camera case** is colored black so that no unwanted light reaches the film.

The **shutter** is like a small gate that opens to let in the light and then closes again. Adjustable shutter speed allows the gate to remain open for different lengths of time.

Find out more by looking at pages **26–27**

The **focus setting** is turned to alter the position of the lens until the object is in focus. Some cameras focus on an object automatically.

lens

The **lens** refracts light that comes from an object and focuses it as a sharp image on the film. Some cameras also have special lenses, such as wide-angle lenses and telephoto lenses. These lenses let the photographer change the size and depth of the scene.

The **aperture** is the hole that is made when the camera's shutter opens. Light enters through it and forms an image on film. The **diaphragm** adjusts the hole's size to let in different amounts of light.

The speed of light

Nothing we know of can travel faster than light. If an object could travel at the speed of light, it could travel around the world about seven and a half times in one second. The light from the sun, 93 million miles (150 million kilometers) away, takes only about eight minutes to reach the earth. A vehicle traveling at 620 miles (1,000 kilometers) per hour would take about 17 years to make the same journey!

Imagine that this boy is a ray of light. He can travel around the world seven and a half times in one second.

How fast does light travel?

In empty space where there is no air, light travels at 186,282 miles (299,792 kilometers) per second. Air slows light down, by about 57 miles (92 kilometers) per second. Glass slows it down much more, to about 122,140 miles (197,000 kilometers) per second.

When light travels through a substance, it slows down only as it passes through the substance. When it reaches the other side, it speeds up again.

As light travels through the lens of your eye, for example, it slows down and is refracted. This means the direction of the light is changed. Astronomers who study the stars through telescopes and photographers who use cameras depend on light to slow down as it travels through a lens.

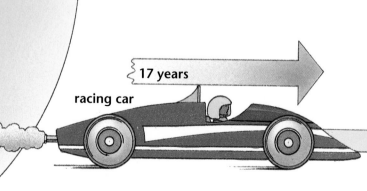

sun

17 years

racing car

This diver shines a beam of light so he can photograph a coral under the water. The beam of light travels more slowly underwater than it would through the air.

If he were a light ray, this boy would take eight minutes to reach the earth from the sun. The racing car, even if it traveled at 620 miles (1,000 kilometers) an hour, would take 17 years to complete the same journey.

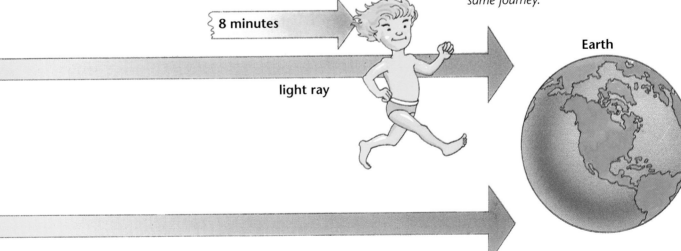

8 minutes

light ray

Earth

At sunset, the sun is low in the sky. The remaining rays of sunlight are orange and red, making the sky an orange-red color.

Why does the sky look blue?

What color is the sky? On a sunny day, the sky looks blue. Sometimes, early in the morning and just before sunset, it may look greenish-yellow, or even orange-red.

The sky actually has no color at all. It is a great ocean of air, called the **atmosphere**, which is made up of colorless gases. The sky looks colored to us because of what happens to the sunlight which passes through the atmosphere.

Scattered light

All kinds of particles, including air molecules, dust, smoke, and ash, float in the air. Many of these particles come from human activities, such as burning fuels to provide energy. Other particles are the result of natural happenings. Strong winds may whip up particles of desert sand. When volcanoes erupt, they send clouds of smoke and ash into the air.

When light strikes the tiny particles that are found in air and water, the light is scattered in all directions. The light waves with the shorter wavelengths—violet and blue—are scattered more easily than those with the longer wavelengths—orange and red. When the sun is overhead, the waves of blue light are scattered much more than those of any other color. That is why the sky appears blue. When the sky is full of clouds or smoke, the light waves of all colors are scattered, and the sky appears gray.

sun

39

Find out more by looking
at pages **24–25**

The rising and setting sun

At sunrise and sunset, rays of sunlight must travel farther through the atmosphere than when the sun is overhead. Because the sun's rays are refracted, the sun appears larger. The light waves of shorter wavelengths of light (blue and violet) are scattered, but the colors with longer wavelengths (orange and red) travel relatively undisturbed. At these times of day, the sky often turns an orange-red color.

As the sun is setting, its light travels to us across Earth's atmosphere. Blue and violet light are gradually scattered. Red and orange light travel through the atmosphere.

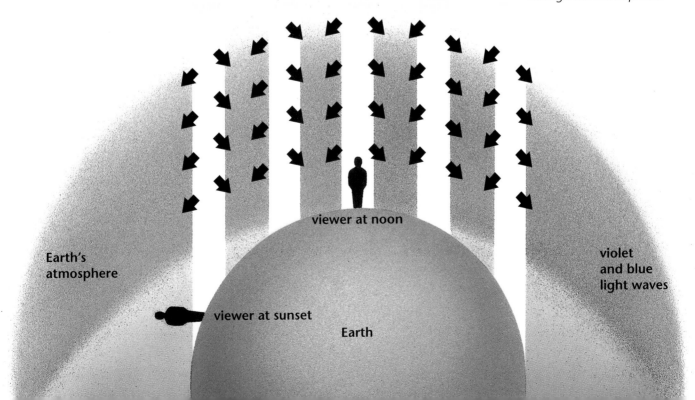

viewer at noon

Earth's atmosphere

viewer at sunset

Earth

violet and blue light waves

Find out more by looking at pages **24–25**

What is a laser?

Did you know that light rays can cut through a steel plate? What sort of light can do this? The answer is **laser light.** A laser can produce a thin but very powerful beam of light.

Ordinary white light is made up of many different colors. Its photons have many different wavelengths. They are out of step with each other. In a beam of laser light, all the photons have the same wavelength and move in step, traveling along like a well-drilled army.

How does a laser work?

A typical laser has three parts: an energy source, an active medium, and an optical cavity. The optical cavity encloses the active medium and two mirrors. One mirror reflects only part of the light striking it.

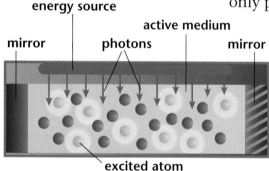

1. When the laser is turned on, the energy source gives off photons. The atoms in the optical cavity absorb the photons, and their energy level increases. Atoms in this state are said to be excited.

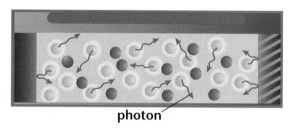

2. Excited atoms give off photons. Some of this light reflects off the mirrors and stays inside the optical cavity.

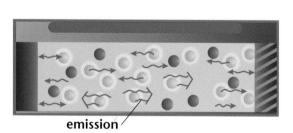

3. A photon shining on an excited atom causes the atom to give off a "twin" photon that travels in the same direction. This process is called stimulated **emission.**

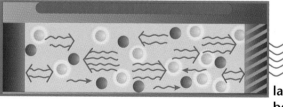

4. As stimulated emission increases, the photons multiply millions of times. The light becomes so strong that a small part of it escapes through the partly reflecting mirror as a strong, narrow beam.

An outdoor laser light show is an entertaining and exciting way to use lasers.

The power of lasers

A laser beam doesn't spread out like a beam of ordinary light. Its energy is concentrated into a narrow width. Some laser beams are thin enough to drill 200 holes in a spot as tiny as the head of a pin.

A laser beam is very powerful. The world's most powerful laser, called Petawatt, produced more than 1 quadrillion (1,000 trillion) watts of power in less than 500 quadrillionths of a second!

Lasers can do many amazing things. They are used to record music, motion pictures, and computer data on special discs. At supermarket counters, laser scanners read the bar code on products. Surgeons use laser light to perform very delicate operations.

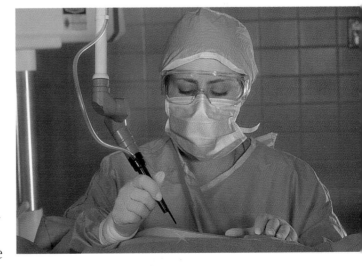

Surgeons use laser light to perform delicate operations.

People also use lasers to measure distances. Geologists use them to detect small movements in the ground, which can help them tell when an earthquake is coming.

Find out more by looking at pages **40–41**

Holograms can be very realistic. You can look at them from any angle. But if you tried to touch one, your hand would pass right through the beam of laser light!

Three-dimensional pictures

Have you ever seen a picture that seems to move when you turn it or move around it? In these pictures, birds seem to fly, or objects seem to spin. Your parents may have a credit card with this kind of special picture on it. You might also see them in advertising displays. These three-dimensional pictures are called **holograms.**

Holograms show an object in its three dimensions—its depth, its length, and its width. An ordinary picture is two-dimensional and shows only the length and width of an object. Ordinary pictures appear flat.

How a hologram works

To make a hologram, a laser beam is reflected off an object and onto a photographic plate. A second beam also shines on the plate. Where the two beams cross, they make a microscopic pattern of bright and dark stripes.

When a hologram is lit up by a laser beam, it produces a pattern of light rays that still seem to come from the object.

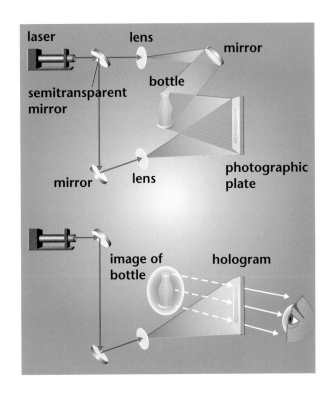

What is a hologram?

A hologram is a special photograph that appears as a three-dimensional picture. It is made using laser light. The word *hologram* means "complete picture." The objects you see in a hologram are very lifelike. They look solid and even look different from different angles—just like real objects.

Normally, your eyes build up separate images of a scene that help you to judge the depth and distance of whatever you are looking at. You can tell which objects are close to you and which ones are in the background.

When a hologram is made, laser light shines onto the object. An image of the object is then recorded onto a special film. Light from the laser also travels directly to the film. The photographic film has to be lit by a laser light or a white light in order for you to view the three-dimensional image of the hologram.

When a hologram is lit up by white light, such as sunlight, it makes an image that seems to move.

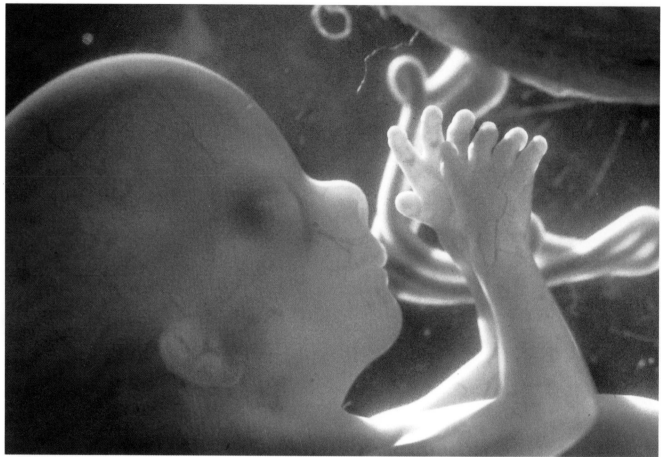

Optical fibers

The baby in the picture on this page hasn't been born yet. It is still lying inside its mother's womb. How could a photograph like this have been taken?

The photograph was taken using flexible, transparent threads, or **fibers**, of glass. These glass threads are called **optical fibers.** They can bend without breaking, like human hairs. If a strong light shines in at one end of an optical fiber, it will shine out at the other end, even if the fiber is several miles long and twisted up like wire! Light travels along the length of the thread at an angle toward the wall of the fiber. It is then reflected back toward the center by plastic coating.

An instrument that uses optical fibers to look inside someone's body is called an **endoscope.** It has two sets of optical fibers—one set carries light to the part of the body being examined, and the other set carries a picture of the area back to the doctor. The photograph of this baby was probably taken to make sure that the baby was developing properly.

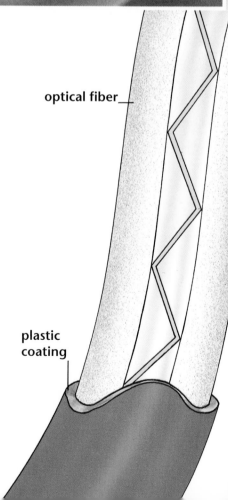

optical fiber

plastic coating

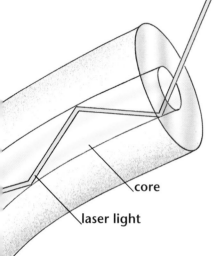

Optical fibers are used to carry radio, telephone, television, and computer data.

core

laser light

What is fiber optics?

The method of using optical fibers to carry images and messages is called **fiber optics.** The fibers are not only used in medicine, but also in communications. Some cable television companies use optical fibers instead of wires to carry sound and picture signals. These signals are changed into bursts, or pulses, of light. Optical fibers are also used by some telephone companies. They are lighter, cheaper, and easier to install than the normal copper cables.

When you speak into a telephone, the sound made by your voice is turned into electric signals which travel down the line. In a fiber optic system, these electric signals are changed again into pulses of laser light. These pulses travel at the speed of light along the fibers. They travel down the fiber until they reach the other end, where they are changed back into electric signals. The signals are then changed again into the sounds that you hear in your telephone earpiece.

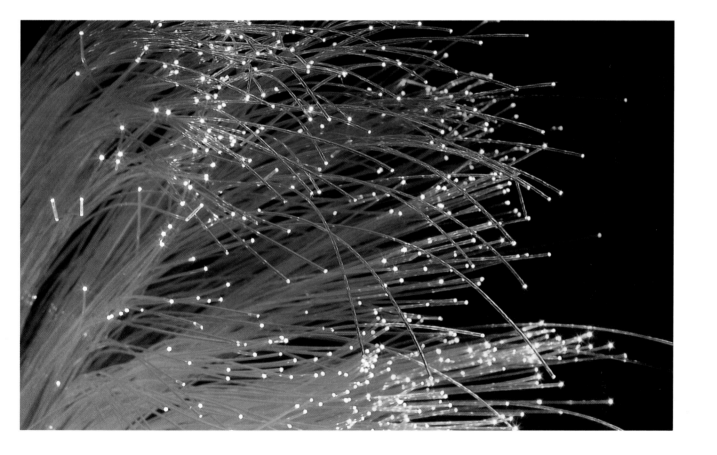

Animals and light

Your view of the world is very different from that of a cat, a dog, an owl, or an insect. Different species of animals have different kinds of eyes to suit the way they live.

Night-hunters

Owls hunt for food at night. They need to make use of all the available light. They must also be able to judge distances accurately so that they can swoop onto their prey. Owls have huge eyes that face forward.

Owls sometimes feed on rabbits. Rabbits have eyes on the sides of their head for an all-around view. They need to keep alert for signs of danger, such as a hunting owl.

When it is dark, the pupils in the owl's eyes are very large, to let in as much light as possible.

Fields of vision

When you look steadily at an object, everything that you see straight ahead of you and to the sides is in your **field of vision.**

Your left eye sees a little more of the left side of the object. Your right eye sees a little more of the right. Your brain blends the left and right views into a single, three-dimensional image. This is called **stereoscopic vision.**

Animals whose eyes are on the sides of their head, such as rabbits, have a large field of vision. They can see almost all around them, which helps them to escape from predators. Humans and some animals, such as owls, have a smaller field of vision because their eyes face forward. But they have better stereoscopic vision.

owl

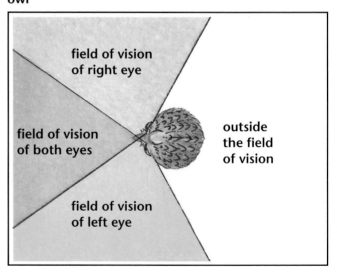

field of vision of right eye

field of vision of both eyes

outside the field of vision

field of vision of left eye

Compound eyes

The eyes of most insects are quite different from ours. Each eye is made up of many tiny lenses set at different angles. The eyes of some insects are made up of thousands of these lenses. This type of eye is called a **compound eye.** Although insects cannot move or focus their eyes, some can see all around them.

Many adult insects also have three **simple eyes** set in a triangle between the compound eyes. Each simple eye has one lens. The simple eyes do not form images, but they respond to light quickly.

The bee also sees ultraviolet light, which is invisible to our eyes. The petals of some flowers, particularly yellow ones, have elaborate patterns which show up under ultraviolet light. These patterns attract the bees to the flowers. Bees are unable to see the color red.

The bee notices moving objects when light or shade moves across different parts of its compound eyes.

rabbit

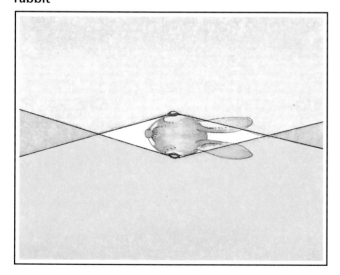

human

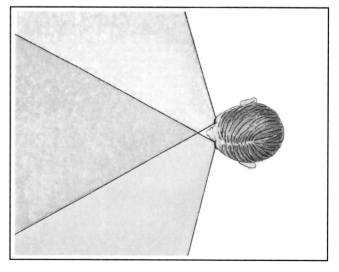

Electricity all around

Have you ever stood outside during a bad storm and seen a sudden flash light up the sky? That was probably lightning. Lightning is very powerful. The heat from a flash of lightning can burn the ground and even set trees or houses on fire. Do you know what lightning is? It's a giant spark of electricity in the air.

Have you ever noticed tiny sparks when you comb your hair, or when you take off a sweater very quickly in the dark? These are sparks of electricity. They are just like lightning flashes, but much smaller and safer.

Living electricity

Your body uses electricity all the time. Your heart produces tiny amounts of electricity to help it beat properly. Your brain is receiving and sending electrical messages to every part of your body, even when you're asleep.

All animals' bodies produce electricity, and some even use it as a weapon. Have you ever heard of the electric eel? The electric eel lives mainly in the Amazon and Orinoco rivers of South America. This eel is a fish that makes its own electricity to help in catching food and in protecting itself against enemies. The eel's body can make enough electricity to kill a small fish or to stun a human being.

Electricity works for us

We don't use electric eels to light up bulbs! Most of the electricity, or electric energy, we use comes from huge power stations.

Can you think of some ways that we use electricity? Electricity lights up bulbs so that we can see at night. Electricity heats up ovens so that we can cook food. Electricity helps to carry our voices along the wires when we speak to people on the telephone. Electric trains take people quickly from one place to another. Electricity makes it possible for computers to do complicated calculations.

Electricity lights up the whole city of Hong Kong at night.

Letting the current flow

Think of 10 objects that are completely different from each other. Make a list. Now here's a surprise! No matter how different the objects on your list are, they all have one very important thing in common. They all contain **electrons.** Electrons are tiny, invisible particles that carry an electric charge.

A flow of electrons is called an **electric current.** An electric current flows easily through some kinds of material, but doesn't flow at all through others. Scientists describe these two different kinds of materials as **conductors** and **insulators.** A material that allows an electric current to flow through it easily is called a conductor. A material that doesn't let an electric current flow through it easily or at all is called a nonconductor, or an insulator.

Tall wooden posts support wires that carry electric current high above the ground. These posts are called telephone poles.

Take a look at a telephone pole if there is one nearby. Can you spot the insulators? What do you think they are made of?

You will need:

three pieces of plastic-coated wire, 8 inches (20 centimeters) long, with bare ends

a screwdriver

masking tape

a 1.5-volt ("D") battery

a 1.5-volt penlight bulb and miniature bulb holder

a collection of objects, such as a toothbrush, pen, ruler, nail, fork, pencil case, thumbtack, and coin

Is it a conductor?

How can you tell which materials are conductors and which are insulators? Find out by setting up a special experiment.

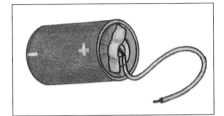

1. Tape the bare end of a piece of wire to the top of the battery.

2. Using the screwdriver, connect the other end of the wire to one of the screws on the bulb holder.

3. Tape one end of the second piece of wire to the bottom of the battery. Do not connect the other end.

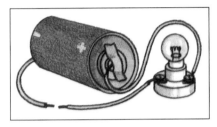

4. Connect one end of the third piece of wire to the other side of the bulb holder. Do not connect the other end.

5. To make sure your equipment works, hold the insulated parts of the two free wires and touch together the two bare ends of wire. The bulb should light up. If you separate the two ends, the bulb should go out. **Do not touch any bare electric wires.**

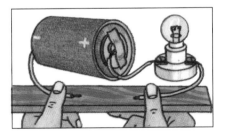

6. Now find out which objects are conductors. Place one bare wire at one end of an object and the second bare wire at the other end. If the bulb lights up, is the object a conductor or an insulator? Do the same with each object.

7. Now write down the names of all those objects that you found to be good conductors. Can you find something that they all have in common? Are all the conductors made from the same type of material?

Around and around the circuit

Do you have a flashlight? Have you ever looked inside it? A flashlight won't light up unless there are **batteries** inside. When you switch it on, the batteries make an electric current flow. This current flows through the bulb and makes it light up.

What is a circuit?

When you switch on a flashlight, the batteries inside create an electric current by making electrons move. The electric current flows out of one end of the battery, through the bulb, and then back into the battery. As long as the current can move freely around this pathway, the bulb will light up. We call this kind of pathway an **electric circuit**. Electrons flow in the direction opposite that of the current.

While the flashlight is switched on, the current continues to flow around and around the circuit. Turning the switch off makes a break in the circuit. Now the current can't flow, and the light goes out.

In this book, you will be using batteries to make electricity. This electricity moves in only one direction around the circuit. We call this kind of electricity **direct current** (or DC) **electricity.**

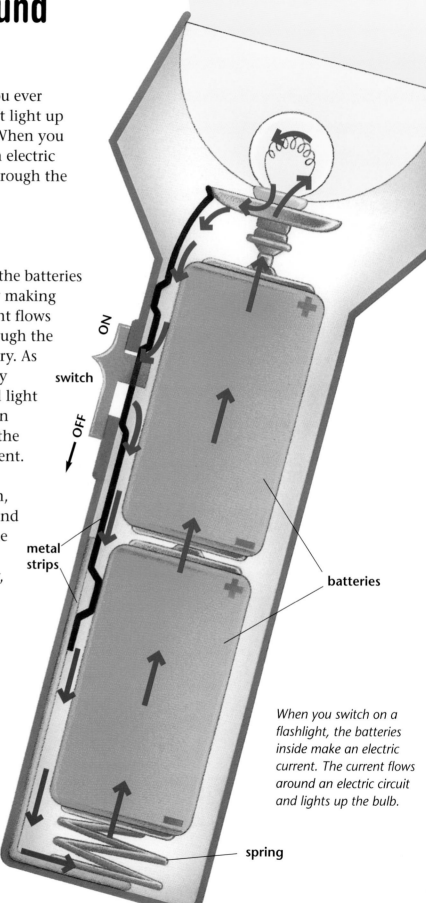

switch

ON

OFF

metal strips

batteries

spring

When you switch on a flashlight, the batteries inside make an electric current. The current flows around an electric circuit and lights up the bulb.

Positive and negative terminals

A battery has two connections where the electric current flows in or out. These connections are called **terminals.** Sometimes, as in most flashlight batteries, the terminals are on either end of the battery. Other batteries have both terminals on one end. One terminal is marked **+** (plus). The other terminal is marked **−** (minus). The electric current flows out of the terminal marked minus, the negative terminal. The current flows into the terminal marked plus, the positive terminal.

You will need:

two pieces of plastic-coated wire, about 8 inches (20 centimeters) long, with bare ends

a screwdriver

masking tape

a 1.5-volt ("D") battery

a 1.5-volt penlight bulb
and miniature bulb holder

Which bulb will light up?

An electric current won't flow if it can't make a complete trip around a circuit. You can test this for yourself. Set up the simple circuits shown below. Can you guess which one will make the bulb light up?

1. Tape one end of a piece of wire to the top battery terminal. Connect the other end of this wire to one side of the bulb holder. Does the bulb light up?

2. Now connect the other circuits shown here. Which one is a complete circuit?

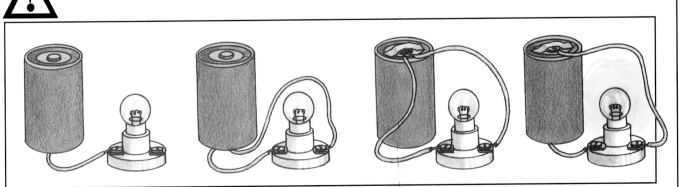

Inside the battery

Do you know how batteries make flashlights and other things work? When you switch on a flashlight, an electric current flows out of the battery, through the flashlight bulb and back into the battery. A battery is made of particular metals and chemicals, which produce the electric current. When these metals and chemicals are put together, they make a **cell.** A battery may have just one cell or more than one. Many flashlight batteries, like the one pictured at left, have one cell. Each cell is made up of three main parts.

Two of the battery parts are solid. These two solid parts are called the electrodes. In an alkaline battery, one electrode is the zinc case. This is the negative electrode. The other electrode is a manganese dioxide rod running down through the middle of the battery. This is the positive electrode. The third part is a chemical liquid or paste, called the electrolyte, a substance that conducts electricity. This is placed between the two electrodes.

When the battery is connected into a circuit, the current flows out of the battery through the bottom of the battery, the negative terminal. The current flows back into the battery through the top of the carbon rod, the positive terminal. Electrically charged atoms in the electrolyte move inside the battery to complete the circuit.

As the current flows through the battery, the chemicals gradually change. They become weaker and have less energy to make electricity. Gradually the battery starts to run down.

A zinc-carbon battery is less expensive than an alkaline battery, but it does not last as long. It uses a different electrolyte.

manganese dioxide rod (positive electrode)

brass cap

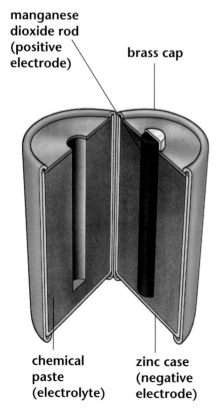

chemical paste (electrolyte)

zinc case (negative electrode)

An alkaline flashlight battery has a zinc case with a manganese dioxide rod running through the middle. The zinc case and the manganese dioxide rod are the two electrodes. The rest of the battery is filled with a chemical called an electrolyte. The entire battery is encased in a paper or metal jacket.

55

Find out more by looking
at pages **52–53**

*Always handle batteries carefully.
Make sure the voltage is correct for
what you are using.*

Have you heard of rechargeable batteries? These differ in
makeup from zinc-carbon and alkaline batteries.
Rechargeable batteries have what are called reversible
chemical reactions. When they wear down, a charger device
can restore power to the batteries by reversing the discharge
of energy that has taken place, reversing the chemical
reaction that produces electricity, and making the batteries
usable again. Rechargeable batteries can last for years, and
they are often recommended as a way to cut down on
having to buy and dispose of too many batteries.

No matter which kind of batteries you use, always handle
them carefully. Make sure the voltage is correct for what you
are using, and have an adult check if you're not sure.

Positive and negative charges

There are two kinds of electrical charges—**positive** and **negative**. An object that gains electrons has a negative charge. An object that loses electrons has a positive charge. Two charges of the same kind push each other apart. We say that they **repel** each other. Two charges of different kinds pull each other together. We say that they **attract** each other.

Try combing your hair quickly, and then holding the comb near your hair. Your hair stands on end! When you combed your hair, electrons rubbed off the hair onto the comb. This set up an electrical charge. The comb gained extra electrons and so had a negative charge. Your hair lost some electrons and so had a positive charge. Your hair rose towards the comb because the positive and negative charges attracted each other.

You will need:

a strip of newspaper 12 inches (30 centimeters) × 2 inches (5 centimeters)

a piece of wool cloth

a plastic ruler

Electron charges

A strip of paper can show you how charges of the same kind repel each other. Try this experiment when the weather is dry and not humid.

1. Stroke the strip of newspaper about 20 times with the piece of cloth.

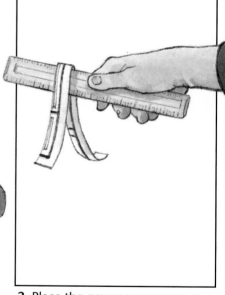

2. Place the newspaper across a plastic ruler and lift up the ruler.

3. What can happen? What does happen? Explain.

A flash of lightning

Lightning happens when positive and negative charges move towards each other through the air. They make an electric current that causes a spark. This spark is the flash of lightning you see during a storm.

1. Before the storm, raindrops and ice particles inside the cloud contain equal numbers of positive and negative charges.

2. As the storm begins, the rain and ice particles inside the cloud bang into each other and the charges are forced apart.

3. Most of the positive charges rise to the top of the cloud and most of the negative charges move to the bottom.

4. Lightning can occur when the negative charges from the cloud meet positive charges rising from the ground. There are also other types of lightning.

Find out more by looking at pages **50–51**

Along the wire

Do you know how water gets to the faucets on your kitchen sink? It comes through pipes. Pipes let water flow in the direction we want it to go.

How do we make electricity flow in the direction we want it to go? The electrical energy we call "electricity" is made in huge **power stations.** What connects the electric **sockets** in your home with the power station? The answer is **wires.** Wires are the "pipes" of the electricity system.

All shapes and sizes

A wire is a long, thin piece of metal. It may be a single **strand** of metal, or it may be two or more strands twisted together. Some wires are thick and stiff, and others are thin and bend easily.

*Wires can be different colors, sizes, and shapes. The colored plastic or rubber that covers all these wires is called **insulation.***

Why are electric wires covered?

A material that allows electricity to flow through it is called a conductor. Metals are good conductors. Some metals are better conductors than others. Silver is the best conductor of all, but it is too expensive to use to make wires. Copper is also a very good conductor and much cheaper to use than silver. So most of the wires that we use to conduct electricity are copper wires.

But it's best not to try to conduct electricity along a bare wire. When a current is flowing through a bare wire, it will also flow through any metal object or other conductor that touches the wire. Even the human body can conduct electricity. If a person standing on the ground touches a bare wire which is connected to a power line, an electric current will flow through the person and into the ground. The person may receive a dangerous electric shock and might even be killed.

We need to make sure that electric current goes just where we want it and nowhere else. So the wires used to carry electricity are covered with materials that are poor conductors of electricity. Rubber and plastic conduct electricity poorly. They are both good insulators. A bare wire that is covered with rubber or plastic is called an **insulated wire**, or **cable.**

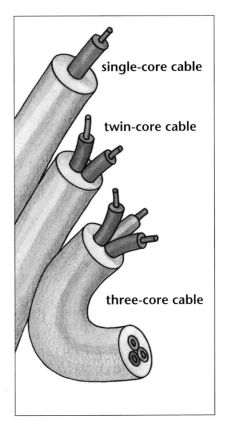

single-core cable

twin-core cable

three-core cable

*If cable is used for the circuit wires, there are three wires inside the cable. Two of these wires carry the electric current to and from the fuse box. One is a black, red, or blue wire and the other a white wire. The third wire, which can be bare or green, is called the **ground wire.** It may be connected to the main water pipe. If there is a fault in the wiring, the ground wire takes the current safely away into the ground.*

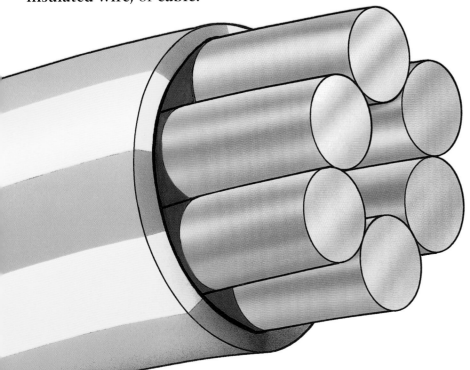

A bare wire that is covered with rubber or plastic is called an insulated wire, or cable. Inside a single cable there may be six or more separate strands of wire.

Measuring in volts

You can make a bulb light up by using two wires to join it to a battery. The bulb lights up because an electric current is flowing through it. The battery produces the current by pushing and pulling electrons along the wires. The stronger the "pushing" and "pulling," the more electrons flow along the wire each second. The current heats the thin wire inside the bulb and makes it glow.

The strength of this push and pull is measured in **volts.** The word *volts* comes from the name of the Italian who invented the first battery—Alessandro Volta. The more volts a battery has, the stronger its push and pull.

How many volts?

When we do experiments with electricity, we use small batteries with a strength of 1.5, 6.0, or 9.0 volts. This **voltage** is printed on the side of the battery.

The voltage of the power line to your home is much higher. The voltage of the electric current flowing through the wires in most homes is at least 110 volts and may be as high as 220 or 240 volts. A voltage of more than 100 volts is enough to push electrons through your body. If a strong electric current passes through your body, the shock will hurt you badly and could easily kill you. **So you must always use low-voltage batteries for your electrical experiments.**

In a copper wire (A), some electrons move freely in all directions. When a battery is connected to the wire (B), the battery "pushes" and "pulls" the electrons in one direction. The flow of electrons this produces is an electric current.

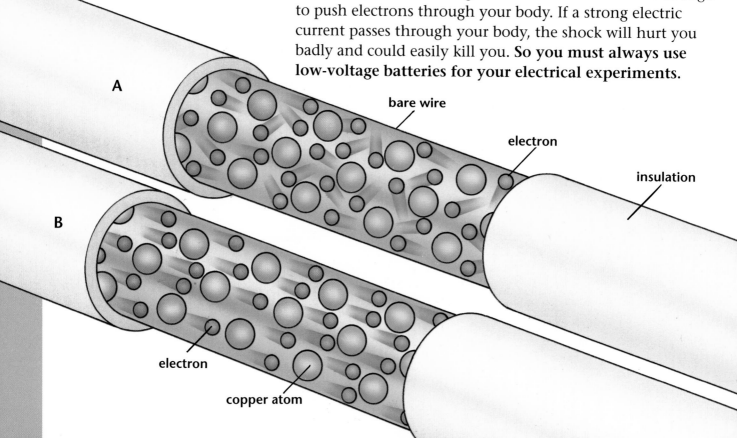

A

B

bare wire

electron

insulation

electron

copper atom

You will need:

three pieces of plastic-coated wire, 8 inches (20 cm) long, with bare ends

two 1.5-volt ("D") batteries

bulb holder

6-volt flashlight bulb

a screwdriver

masking tape

Using more volts

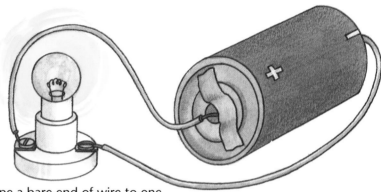

1. Tape a bare end of wire to one terminal of the battery. Tape the end of another wire to the other terminal. Connect the two free ends of wire to the bulb holder. The bulb will light up.

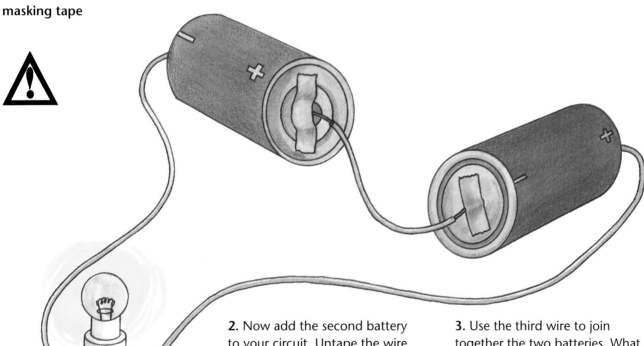

2. Now add the second battery to your circuit. Untape the wire from the negative terminal of the first battery. Tape it to the negative terminal on the second battery.

3. Use the third wire to join together the two batteries. What happens now? Does the bulb shine with the same brightness? Or more brightly? Or less brightly? Explain.

How many amps?

Most electrical appliances have wires attached to them. The wires carry an electric current around a complete pathway called an electric circuit. Some appliances need more electric current than others before they will work. The amount of electric current depends on how much electricity is flowing along the wires.

Measuring electric current

How can we measure the amount of electric current? We could try counting the number of electrons that pass along the wire each second. But this wouldn't be easy! There are a huge number of electrons traveling along most electric wires. About 3 million million million electrons flow through a flashlight bulb every second!

To make it easier, we measure the flow of electric current in **amperes.** The word *ampere* comes from the name of the French scientist André Ampère, who invented a way of measuring electric current. We usually say *amp* instead of *ampere.* One amp is equal to about 6 million million million electrons every second. So a flashlight bulb would have a current of half an amp flowing through it. That's much easier!

Scientists use a special measuring device called a **multimeter** to measure electric current, voltage, and resistance. The multimeter is connected to an electric circuit so that the electrons flowing around the circuit also flow through the multimeter.

The bulb from your experiments needs only about 0.3 amp to make it light up. But the welding equipment used in heavy industry requires hundreds of amps.

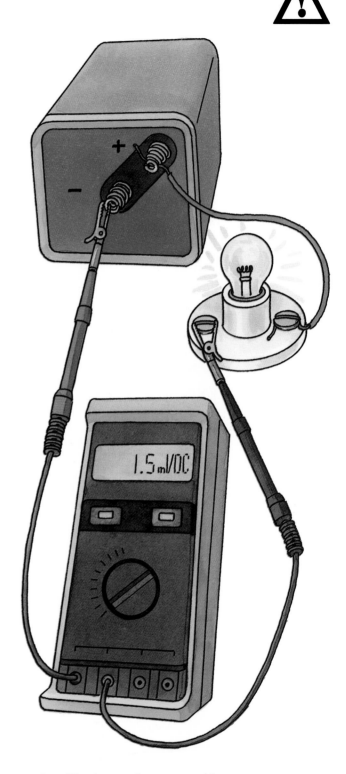

A multimeter can be connected in a simple electric circuit. The electrons flowing around the circuit flow through the multimeter, as well as through the bulb and the battery.

Find out more by looking
at pages **52–53**

*An electric current of between 50 and 300 amps
provides the heat needed to weld together pieces of
steel. This method of welding is called arc welding.*

Heating up

Do you know what makes a light bulb light up? Look closely at a transparent light bulb and you'll see a coil of thin wire. This coil of wire is made from a metal named tungsten and is called a **filament**. When an electric current passes through a filament, it gets hot and glows brightly.

Why does the filament get hot? As the electrons flow along the wire, they give off energy in the form of heat. This heat is trapped in the wire. The heat makes the filament glow so that it produces light.

Thin wires, thick wires

Electrons lose energy because wire resists the flow of electrons along it. This lost energy gets trapped in the wire and heats it up. A thin wire resists the electrons more than a thick wire made of the same material. So it's easier for electrons to flow along a thick wire than along a thin wire. Scientists say that a thin wire has a higher **resistance** than a thick wire.

The filament of coiled tungsten in a light bulb has a high resistance. Electrons passing through it lose a lot of energy. This trapped energy turns into heat and light.

The light bulb contains a coil of thin wire called a filament. The more wire in a coil, the more light is produced.

Inside a light bulb there is a thin coil of a metal called tungsten. This coil gets very hot and gives off light when an electric current passes through it.

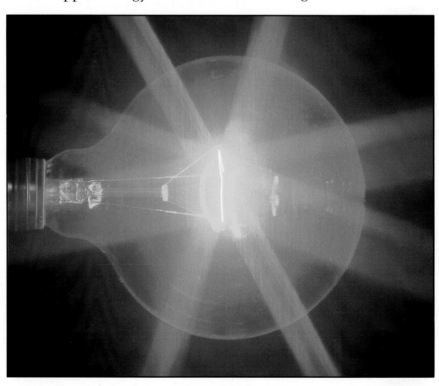

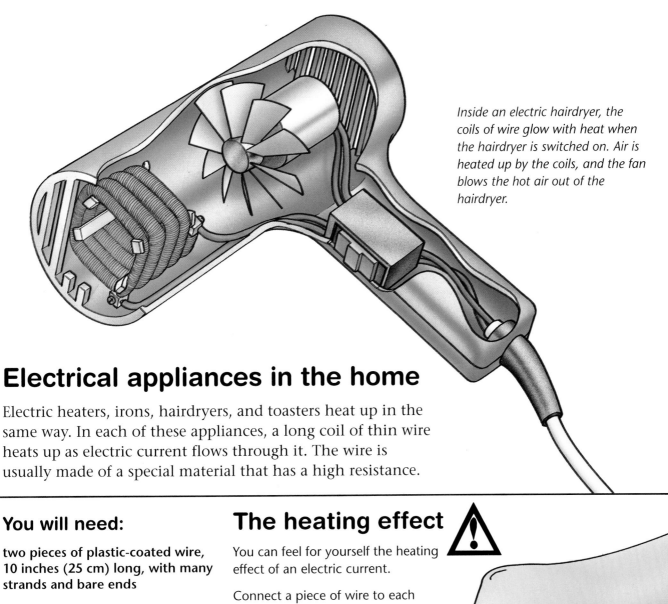

Inside an electric hairdryer, the coils of wire glow with heat when the hairdryer is switched on. Air is heated up by the coils, and the fan blows the hot air out of the hairdryer.

Electrical appliances in the home

Electric heaters, irons, hairdryers, and toasters heat up in the same way. In each of these appliances, a long coil of thin wire heats up as electric current flows through it. The wire is usually made of a special material that has a high resistance.

You will need:

two pieces of plastic-coated wire, 10 inches (25 cm) long, with many strands and bare ends

a 6-volt battery

The heating effect

You can feel for yourself the heating effect of an electric current.

Connect a piece of wire to each terminal of the battery. Separate a single strand at the end of each wire. Now squeeze together the two strands between your thumb and forefinger. You will soon feel the wires start to heat up at the point where you are squeezing them together.

Make sure that you use an ordinary 6-volt lantern battery for this experiment. **Don't use a high-power battery because it will make the wires too hot and you could burn your fingers.**

Switching on and off

A **switch** is a way of turning an electric current on and off. When a switch is turned off, the electric circuit is broken. No electric current can flow around the circuit. When a switch is turned on, the circuit is complete and the current can flow.

You will need:

a small block of soft wood, about 3 inches × 2 inches × ¹/₂ inch (7.5 cm × 5 cm × 1.25 cm)

three pieces of plastic-coated wire, each about 10 inches (25 cm) long, with bare ends

bulb holder

a 6-volt flashlight bulb

a 6-volt battery

a screwdriver

paper clip

two thumbtacks

Making a switch

You can make a simple switch to use in your experiments.

1. Attach a piece of wire to each thumbtack. Push one thumbtack into one of the flat sides of the wood. Push the second thumbtack through the end loop of the paper clip and into the wood. The thumbtacks should be about ¹/₂ inch (1.25 cm) apart.

Make sure the clip is held in place by one thumbtack but can still turn around and touch the other. This is the switch.

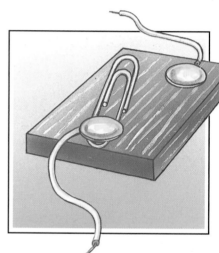

2. To test the switch, connect the free end of one of the wires to one of the battery terminals. Connect the third wire to the other battery terminal and to the bulb holder.

Connect the free wire on the switch to the free screw on the bulb holder.

Turn the paper clip around so that it is touching both thumbtacks. What happens? Now turn the paper clip away from the free thumbtack. What happens?

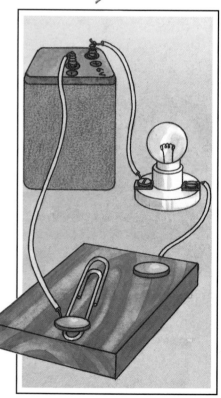

What is a short circuit?

If the plastic covering that insulates a wire wears through, and two bare wires touch, the electric current can pass directly from one wire to the other. This causes what we call a **short circuit**.

Find out more by looking at pages **68–69**

Making a short circuit

You will need:

three pieces of bare wire, about 10 inches (25 cm) long

a 1.5-volt battery

a 1.5-volt penlight bulb and holder

a screwdriver

masking tape

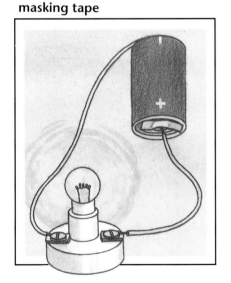

1. Connect the bulb to the battery using two pieces of wire. The bulb will shine brightly.

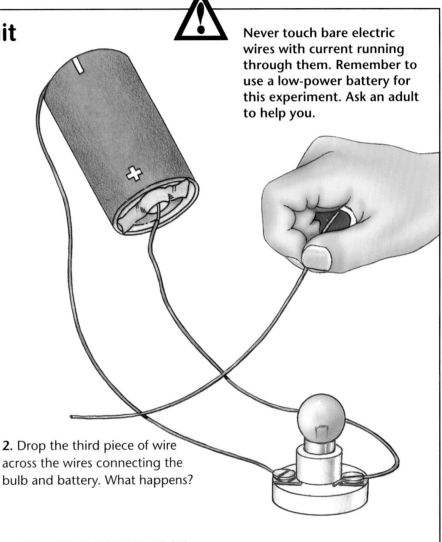

Never touch bare electric wires with current running through them. Remember to use a low-power battery for this experiment. Ask an adult to help you.

2. Drop the third piece of wire across the wires connecting the bulb and battery. What happens?

The extra wire has caused a short circuit. The current is flowing through this wire rather than through the bulb. The current flows more easily through the thick wire, which has less resistance, than through the thin filament of the bulb.

You can also make the bulb go out by joining your third piece of wire into the circuit. Can you find a way of doing this?

Making electricity safe

If something goes wrong with the electrical wiring in your home, it can be very dangerous. For instance, when two bare wires in a circuit touch each other, a short circuit occurs and the wires heat up. The overheated wires could cause a fire.

Circuits and fuses

To make sure that wires don't overheat, most electrical circuits have a device that can break the circuit. The two main devices are the **fuse** and the **circuit breaker**.

Fuses help to make electricity safe to use. A fuse is a thin piece of metal wire that melts more easily than other wires. Some household circuits have two types of fuses. In a fuse box, the fuses are thin, bare wires. In an electrical plug, the fuse is shaped like a small cylinder. The fuse wire is inside the cylinder, or cartridge. This type of fuse is called a cartridge fuse. If the wires in a circuit start heating up, the fuse will quickly melt and cause a break in the circuit.

Circuit breakers protect the wiring in homes and other buildings. If too many electrical devices are plugged into an outlet, a circuit breaker will shut off the current by throwing open its switches. The switch can then be closed again to restore electricity.

cartridge fuses

Do not play with regular electricity in your house!

You will need:

four pieces of plastic-coated wire, 8 inches (20 cm) long, with bare ends

some fine steel wool

a 6-volt battery

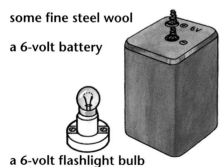

a 6-volt flashlight bulb
bulb holder

a screwdriver

How a fuse works

1. Connect one piece of wire to one terminal of the battery. Connect the other end of the wire to one side of the bulb holder.

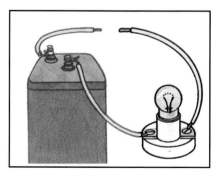

2. Connect the second piece of wire to the other side of the bulb holder. Connect the third piece of wire to the other terminal of the battery.

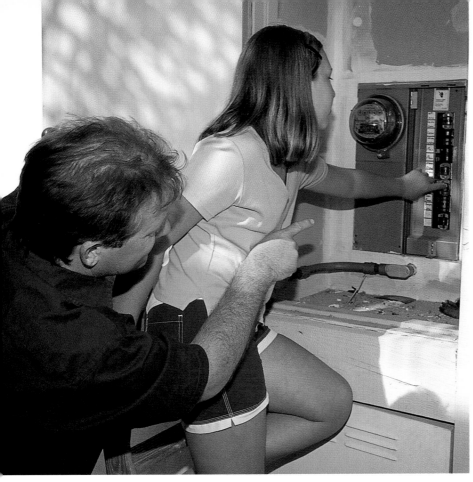

Somewhere in your home—probably in your basement, if you have one—there is a large box that contains several circuit breakers. Circuit breakers protect the wiring in homes and other buildings. If too many electrical devices are plugged into an outlet, a circuit breaker will shut off the current by throwing open its switches. The switch can then be closed again to restore electricity. In a fuse box, the fuses in which the wires melted must be replaced.

Some modern electrical plugs have a cartridge fuse inside. A number stamped on a fuse tells you how many amps can flow through the fuse before it will melt.

Do not ever open a fuse box or touch a circuit breaker without adult supervision.

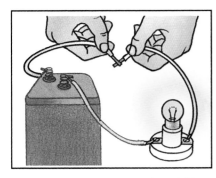
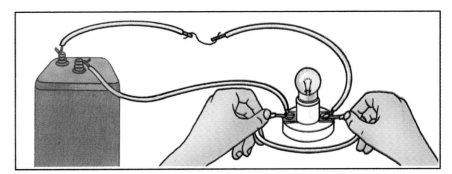

3. Test your apparatus by picking up the two free wires by the plastic coating. Touch the bare ends together, **without touching them with your hands,** and the bulb should light up. Separate the two ends and the bulb should go out.

4. Disconnect the third wire from the battery while you connect a thin strand of steel wool to the other two free ends of wire. The strand of steel wool is now your fuse. Reconnect the third wire to the battery to complete your circuit. Then place the bare ends

of the fourth piece of wire on the two screws of the bulb holder. What happens?

The bulb will go out. The steel wool quickly heats up and melts. This breaks the circuit and the current stops flowing.

Generating electricity

Most of the electricity we use in our homes comes from large power stations. Cables and wires carry the electric current to towns and cities, and to wherever else it is needed. Inside the power stations, there are huge rotating wheels called **turbines.** These turbines are attached to electric generators. Each turbine is made of curved blades, like the sails of a windmill. Hot steam flows over the blades. When the blades spin around, they turn a shaft attached to the generator. As the shaft turns, the generator produces electrical energy.

The steam that turns the turbine is made by heating water in a boiler. Some power stations heat the water by burning fossil fuels, such as coal, oil, or natural gas. **Nuclear power stations** use fuels such as uranium to heat the water. Uranium does not burn like coal or oil. Instead it changes into other substances, and creates heat in the process. The heat is then used to produce the steam to run the turbines.

This cut-away view of the turbines inside a power station shows the huge blades inside. The generator is attached to one end of the turbines.

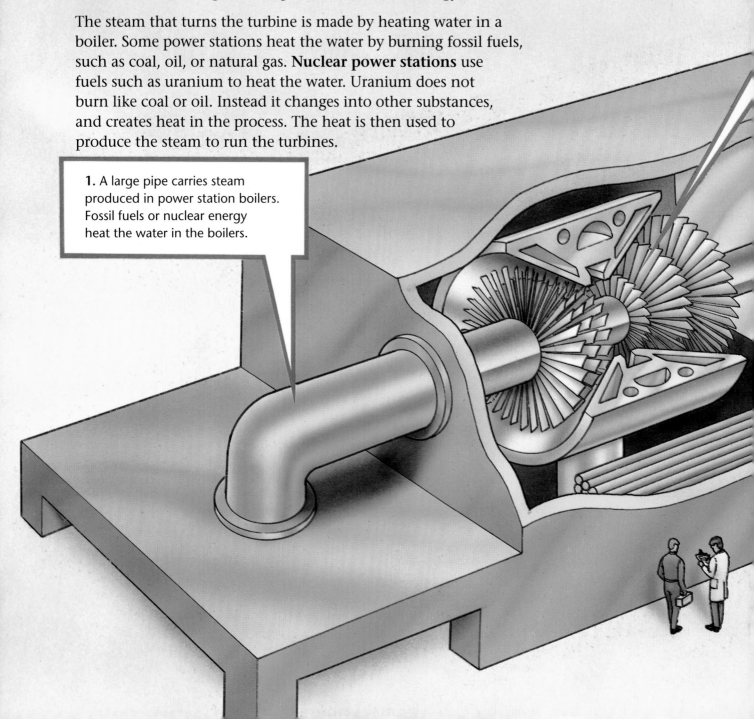

1. A large pipe carries steam produced in power station boilers. Fossil fuels or nuclear energy heat the water in the boilers.

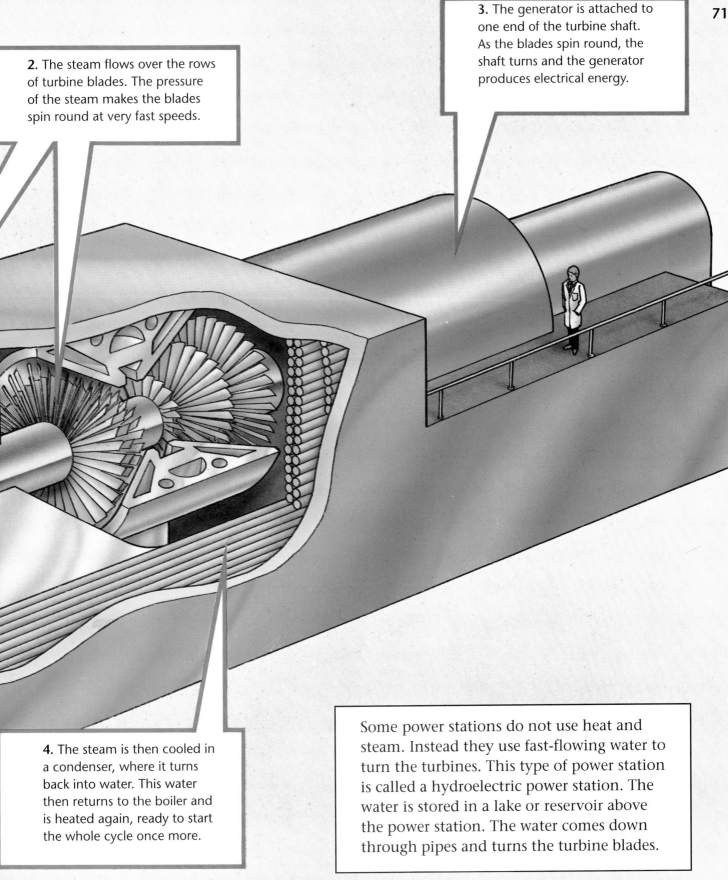

2. The steam flows over the rows of turbine blades. The pressure of the steam makes the blades spin round at very fast speeds.

3. The generator is attached to one end of the turbine shaft. As the blades spin round, the shaft turns and the generator produces electrical energy.

4. The steam is then cooled in a condenser, where it turns back into water. This water then returns to the boiler and is heated again, ready to start the whole cycle once more.

Some power stations do not use heat and steam. Instead they use fast-flowing water to turn the turbines. This type of power station is called a hydroelectric power station. The water is stored in a lake or reservoir above the power station. The water comes down through pipes and turns the turbine blades.

72

Find out more by looking
at pages **50–51**
    60–61
    66–67

What is a transformer?

A transformer can make an electric current smaller or larger. As an electric current flows along the wires from a power station, it loses energy. A large current loses much more energy than a small current.

So power stations use transformers to reduce the current. Transformers do this by increasing the voltage. When the voltage is increased, the current becomes smaller. A transformer that increases the voltage is called a **step-up transformer**.

Many household appliances, such as radios and battery chargers, also use transformers. The voltage these appliances need is lower than the voltage of the electricity in your home. A transformer that reduces the voltage is called a **step-down transformer**.

How do transformers work?

A transformer contains an iron core with two coils of wire wrapped around it. These two coils of wire have a different number of turns. Alternating current flows separately through each coil. In a step-up transformer, the second coil has more turns of wire than the first coil. The voltage of the second coil is then higher than the voltage of the first coil.

In a step-down transformer, the second coil has fewer turns of wire. The voltage of the second coil is then lower than the voltage of the first coil.

Alternating current passes through the first coil in this step-up transformer. This makes an electric current flow in the second coil, which has more turns of wire. The voltage of the second coil is higher than the voltage of the first coil.

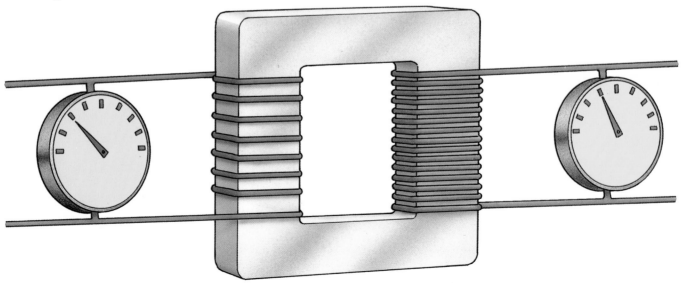

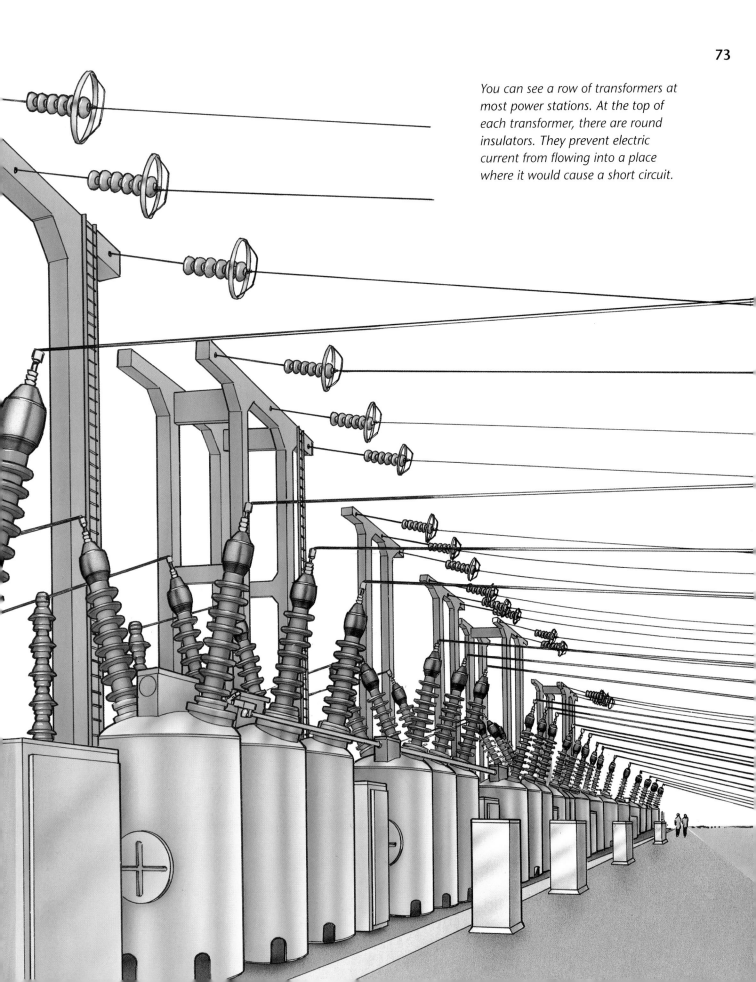

You can see a row of transformers at most power stations. At the top of each transformer, there are round insulators. They prevent electric current from flowing into a place where it would cause a short circuit.

Living without electricity

Before scientists discovered how to generate electricity, people had to use other sources of energy. For centuries, people burned wood or coal to heat their homes and cook their food. They built windmills and waterwheels that used the power of the wind and of water.

Today, many power stations burn fossil fuels, such as coal, oil, or natural gas to produce electricity. But fossil fuels produce a great deal of pollution. What's more, we may run out of them some day.

Other power stations turn nuclear energy into electricity. But many people are concerned about nuclear power stations because of the dangerous materials they use and produce.

There is as yet no source of energy that is practical, clean, safe, and not in danger of running out some day. We still have to look for alternative ways of producing the energy we need.

A solar panel is fitted on the roof of this house. The panel collects energy from the sun and uses it to heat up water. The hot water flows around the house and can be used for heating and washing.

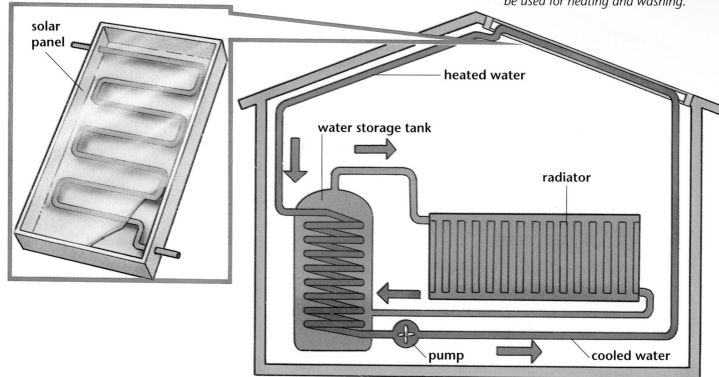

solar panel

heated water

water storage tank

radiator

pump

cooled water

Find out more by looking at pages **70–71**

At this geothermal power station in New Zealand, hot water rises from the ground. When it reaches the surface, it turns to steam, which is used to produce electricity.

For centuries, windmills have used the power of the wind. Long before people began using electricity, windmills were used to grind wheat and corn and run machinery such as pumps. Today, some companies even use high-tech windmills to generate electric power.

Alternative energy

Scientists have found ways to catch energy from the sun, and from the rocks below the ground. Energy from the sun is called **solar energy.** A solar panel can be fitted to the roof of your house to catch this energy. Through the solar panel, the rays heat water that you can use for heating or for washing.

Energy trapped in the hot rocks below Earth's surface is called **geothermal energy.** In some countries, such as Iceland, Italy, Mexico, the Philippines, New Zealand, and the United States, geothermal energy is already being used. Hot rocks inside Earth heat water there. Pumps then bring this water to the surface, where it is piped to homes to heat them.

Scientists are now finding ways of trapping energy from Earth, the sun, and the wind—energy that can, in certain cases, replace electricity as a power source.

MAGNETIC POWER

Magnets all around

We use **magnetism** in so many ways that modern life would be impossible without it. We need magnetism to produce large amounts of electricity in power stations. There are **magnets** in compasses, loudspeakers, electric motors, refrigerator doors, cassette recorders, computer disks, and many other useful appliances. Magnets are also necessary components of machines used in business and industry, such as computers, fax machines, photocopiers, and printing presses.

What is magnetism?

Magnetism is an invisible force that can make some things move towards each other, or move away from each other, or stay in one place. We can't actually see magnetism, but we can look at magnets and see what happens to certain things that are put near them. The area around a magnet is called a **magnetic field.** When magnets and some metals are inside a magnetic field, magnetism makes them move.

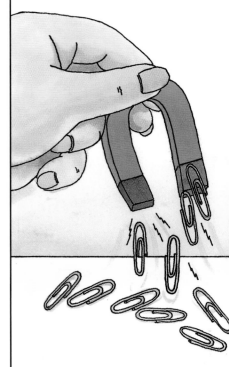

A strong enough magnet can make steel paper clips jump off a table. This is caused by an invisible force, called magnetism, which surrounds every kind of magnet.

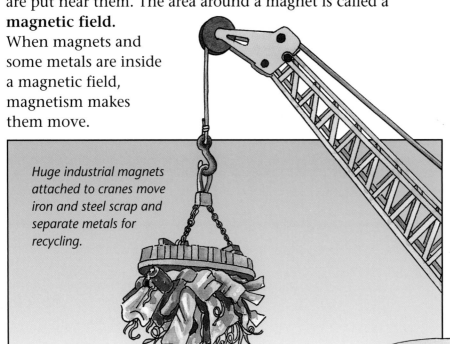

Huge industrial magnets attached to cranes move iron and steel scrap and separate metals for recycling.

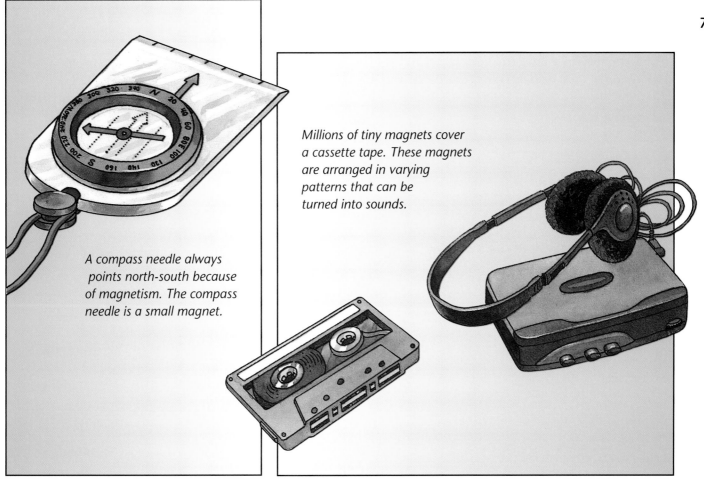

A compass needle always points north-south because of magnetism. The compass needle is a small magnet.

Millions of tiny magnets cover a cassette tape. These magnets are arranged in varying patterns that can be turned into sounds.

Maglev trains use magnetic forces to travel at high speeds. These trains float above a fixed track without touching it. The trains are lifted into the air when magnets under the track are attracted upward to rails under the track.

Radios, cassette players, and televisions send vibrating electric signals into a loudspeaker. Magnetic fields help to change these signals into sounds that we can hear.

Find out more by looking at pages **82–83**

Magnets and materials

When a magnet is surrounded by a magnetic field all the time, we call it a **permanent magnet.** Most permanent magnets are made from steel or from mixtures, called *alloys,* of iron and other metals. Many magnets are made from an alloy called *alnico.* This contains the metals **al**uminum, **ni**ckel, **i**ron and **co**balt. The bold letters show you how we form the name alnico.

Permanent magnets are made of metal and can make other metals move toward them. Scientists describe metals that magnets can attract in this way as **magnetic.** Iron, steel, cobalt, and nickel are magnetic. But not all metals are magnetic. For example, magnets do not attract aluminum or copper. Scientists describe these metals as **nonmagnetic.**

You can find out for yourself whether something is magnetic or nonmagnetic. Hold a small magnet near a piece of paper to see if the paper will move towards the magnet. Now try the same experiment with things made of plastic, glass, and cloth. Are these materials magnetic or nonmagnetic?

Iron filings stick to the ends of a magnet where the magnetic force is strongest. These ends are called the poles of the magnet.

What shape is a magnet?

Magnets are made in several shapes, including bars, horseshoes, rings, disks, and cylinders. Magnetism works in a different way around each shape of magnet. We use bar magnets in compasses, horseshoe magnets in small electric motors, and disk magnets in radio, television, or stereo loudspeakers.

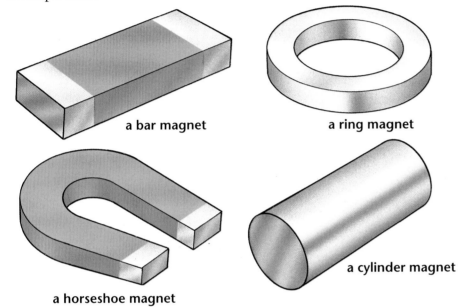

a bar magnet

a ring magnet

a horseshoe magnet

a cylinder magnet

North and south poles

Magnetism is strongest at the ends, or poles, of a bar magnet. Scientists call one end of a bar magnet the **north-seeking pole** because it always tries to point toward the north. The other end is called the **south-seeking pole.** We call them the **north pole** and **south pole** for short.

Do you want to know which end of your bar magnet is the north pole? Find out which direction is north with a compass. Then hang the magnet from a piece of string so that it can swing freely. When it eventually stops swinging, the end of the magnet that points north is the north pole of the magnet.

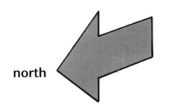

north

Find out more by looking at pages **80–81**

Finding out about poles

If you put a metal object made of iron, steel, cobalt, or nickel near a magnet, the magnet will pull the metal toward it. Scientists say that the magnet **attracts** the metal. Magnets can also attract other magnets, but sometimes magnets push away from each other. Then scientists say that the magnets **repel** each other.

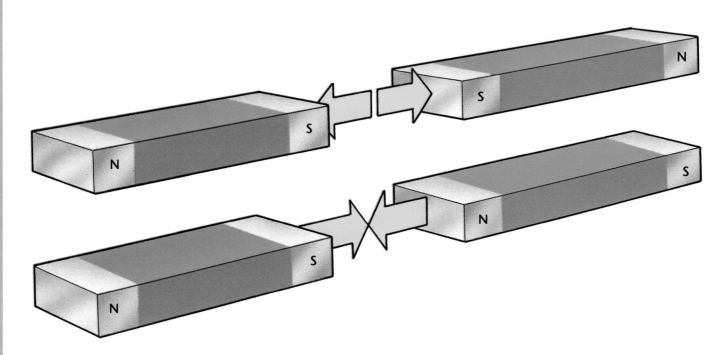

Like and unlike poles

To make a triangle of magnets, each north pole must be next to a south pole. If you try to put two like poles together, the triangle will fall apart.

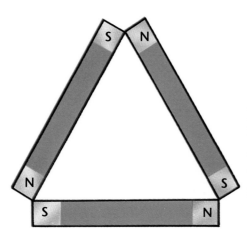

You can feel two magnets attract each other if you hold the north pole of one magnet near the south pole of another magnet. But if you put two poles of the same kind close together, two north poles or two south poles, then the magnets will repel each other. Scientists have a rule to help us remember this. The rule is, "Like poles repel, unlike poles attract."

See this for yourself by making a triangle with three bar magnets. You can't make the magnets stay together if you put two like poles next to each other. The north pole of one magnet, for example, will always repel the north poie of another magnet. If you want your magnets to attract each other and stay close together, the north pole of one magnet must be next to the south pole of the other magnet.

How strong is your magnet?

Some magnets are stronger than others. The force of magnetism is always strongest at the pole of a magnet.

You will need:

several different kinds of magnets

about 20 metal paper clips

1. Pick up one paper clip with a horseshoe magnet. Now put a second paper clip near the first one. It will cling on, because magnetism travels through the first paper clip and attracts the second one.

2. Add more paper clips one at a time to make a chain. How many paper clips can this magnet hold?

3. Try the same experiment with each magnet. Which is the strongest magnet? Are the biggest magnets also the strongest ones?

4. Now find out where the magnetism is strongest on one magnet. Start the chain of paper clips from three different parts of the same bar magnet. Start once with the north pole, once with the south pole, and once in the middle of the magnet. Where is the magnetism strongest?

5. Can you make a chain of paper clips from one pole of a magnet to the other pole?

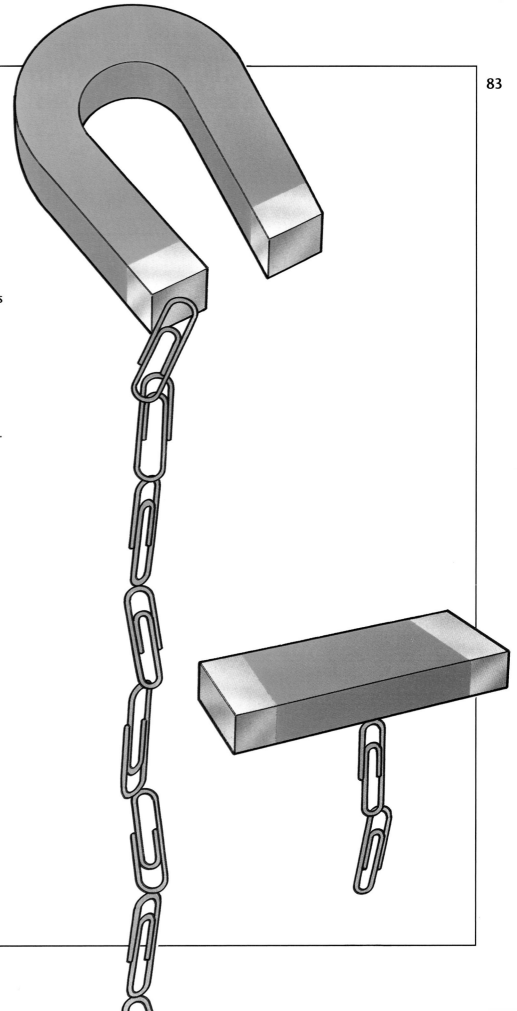

What is a magnetic field?

You can't see magnetism, but you can feel it working near a magnet. In the space around a magnet is a **magnetic field.** If you hold something made from magnetic material, such as iron or steel, in a magnetic field, you can feel the magnet and the metal attract each other even before they touch. If you hold the north pole of one magnet near the north pole of another magnet, you can feel the two magnets repel each other.

You will need:

a large piece of paper

a pencil

a bar magnet

a small compass

Mapping a magnetic field

Although you can't see magnetism, you can make a map of a magnetic field that will help you to see where and how magnetism works.

1. Place the magnet in the middle of a large piece of paper and draw around it in pencil to mark its position.

2. Put the compass near the magnet. Draw a short arrow from the compass to the magnet, showing the direction the needle is pointing.

3. Move the compass to another position. Draw another arrow showing the direction of the needle. Move the compass to about 20 places around the magnet. Draw short arrows in each location.

4. The arrows on your map form curved lines that run from the north pole of the magnet to the south pole. The lines are drawn closer to each other near the poles, where the magnetism is strongest. Away from the poles, where the magnetism is weaker, the lines are drawn farther apart from each other.

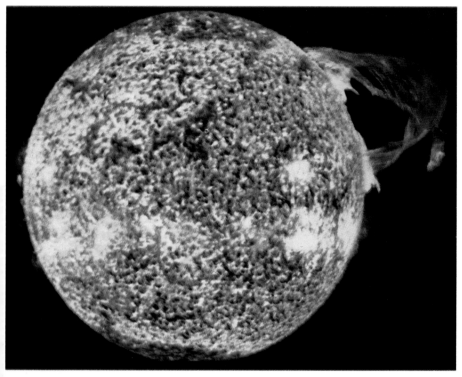

There's a huge magnetic field around the sun. Glowing gases burst out from the sun's surface. These gases help us to see the curved shapes of the sun's magnetic field.

Pulling together or pushing apart?

The shape of a magnetic field changes when you put two magnets together. If you put the north pole of one bar magnet near the south pole of another bar magnet, you can think of their magnetic field as consisting of imaginary lines, called **flux lines**, that pass from one magnet to the other. Between the centers of the poles, the flux lines are straight. Moving away from the centers, the lines curve in ever-expanding arches.

If you put the north poles of two bar magnets close together, there are no flux lines because the magnets repel each other.

When two magnets are end to end, the shape of the magnetic field around them depends on which poles are facing each other. The lines drawn here show how the magnets either attract or repel each other.

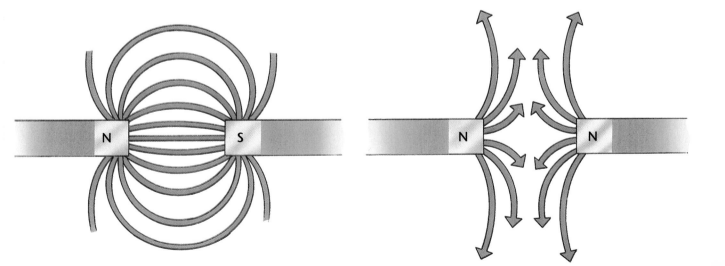

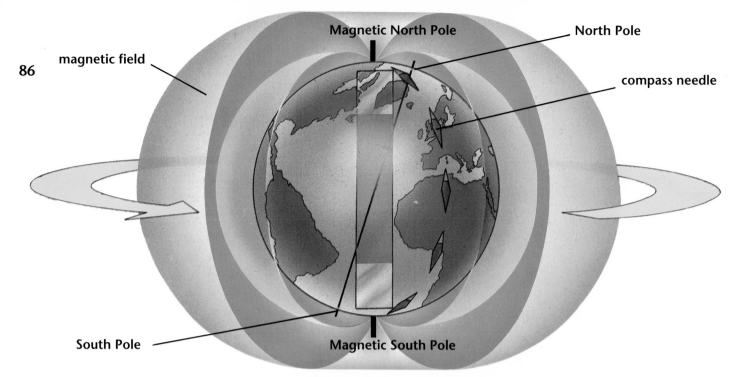

magnetic field

Magnetic North Pole

North Pole

compass needle

South Pole

Magnetic South Pole

A compass needle points towards north and south because Earth is like a huge bar magnet. But Earth's magnetic poles are not exactly the same as the geographic, or true, North and South poles.

Earth's magnetic field

We live on a huge magnet! Around Earth is a giant magnetic field, just like the magnetic field around a bar magnet. Do you know what makes Earth magnetic? Very deep inside Earth, there's hot molten metal. Scientists believe the motion of electric charges in this metal produces the geomagnetic field.

Where are the magnetic poles?

Although Earth is round, it has magnetic poles at two ends just like a bar magnet. Imagine a rod passing through the center of Earth from north to south. One end is the north magnetic pole, and the other end is the south magnetic pole. But the magnetic poles are not in the same places as the North Pole and the South Pole on a geographer's map. These geographic poles are at true north and true south, which are where the earth's lines of longitude meet. But compasses point to the north and south magnetic poles, which are points in Earth's magnetic field.

The north magnetic pole is in Canada, about 870 miles (1,400 kilometers) from the geographic North Pole. The south magnetic pole is in Antarctica, about 1,710 miles (2,750 kilometers) from the geographic South Pole.

Earth's magnetism

We use magnetism to send radio signals across long distances. Earth's magnetism helps to trap a layer of electrical particles around the planet. This layer is called the ionosphere. Radio signals can be sent from the ground to bounce off the ionosphere and return to the ground a great distance from where they started.

Sometimes electrically charged particles erupt from the sun's surface. A stream of these particles sweeps past Earth and interferes with the ionosphere. When this happens, compass needles swing wildly in all directions, and we can't send radio signals across long distances.

Beautifully colored lights can often be seen in the night sky near the North and South poles. These lights are called the aurora, and they are caused by the flow of the particles. The **aurora borealis** in the north and the **aurora australis** in the south appear when these particles get trapped in Earth's magnetic field. Many of these particles travel toward Earth's magnetic poles. Energy is released when the charged particles strike atoms and molecules in Earth's atmosphere, and some of this energy appears in the form of auroras.

The beautiful northern lights, called the aurora borealis, shimmer in the night sky near the North Pole.

Making magnets

You can make a magnet! If you have one magnet already, you can magnetize another piece of metal, such as a steel needle, to make a new magnet. This is how to do it. Hold a steel needle in one hand and a bar magnet in the other hand. Stroke one end, or pole, of the magnet all along the needle several times. You must always use the same pole of the magnet, and stroke the needle in the same direction. In between strokes, lift the magnet in a curve high above the needle from one end to the other. You have now magnetized the needle.

What's inside a magnet?

How does the needle become magnetized? Actually, there were magnets inside the needle even before you stroked it with the magnet. The needle, the magnet, and everything in the world are made up of tiny building blocks called atoms. Atoms are so small that even if you could put a million atoms side by side, a strand of human hair would be thicker. The atoms in a steel needle group together into **domains**, which are magnetized bunches of atoms.

Inside a magnet, all the domains point in the same direction and create a magnetic field around the magnet. But in the steel needle, the domains point in all different directions. There is no magnetic field around the needle because the domains cancel each other out. When you stroke a steel needle with a magnet, you make more and more of the domains line up in the same direction. Then the needle becomes a magnet, too.

⚠ **Be careful with the needle.**

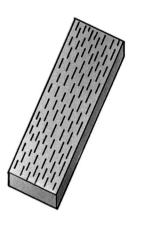

In an ordinary steel or iron bar, the domains are like miniature magnets. They point in many different directions.

When the bar is magnetized, the domains line up in one direction and make a single magnet.

It's easy to make a steel needle into a magnet. Stroke the needle several times with one end of a bar magnet. Make sure you always stroke in the same direction. Always use the same end of the bar magnet.

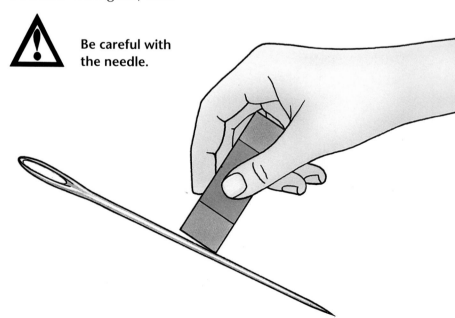

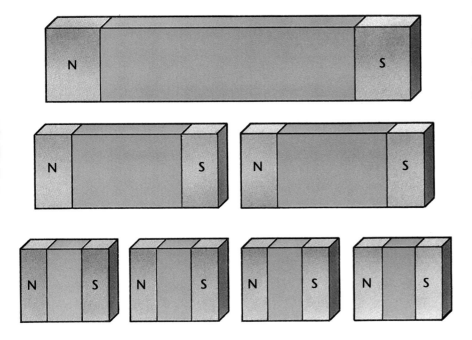

If a magnet is cut in half, it makes two new magnets. Each magnet has a north and a south pole. If each half is then cut in two, there will be four magnets.

Cutting magnets in half

What happens if a bar magnet is cut in half? There will be two magnets! Do you know why? When the magnet is cut in half, the domains are still lined up in each piece. So each half becomes a magnet, with a north pole at one end and a south pole at the other end. If each magnet is cut in half again, there will be four magnets.

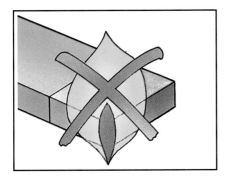

Never heat a magnet. Heat destroys magnetism because it rearranges the domains in all directions.

Don't hit a magnet with a hammer or other hard object. The shock destroys magnetism by rearranging the domains in all directions.

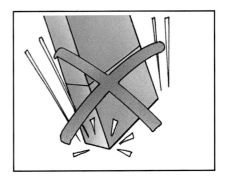

Don't drop a magnet onto the floor. When the magnet hits the floor, the domains will no longer line up and the magnet will lose its magnetism.

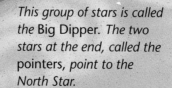

This group of stars is called the Big Dipper. The two stars at the end, called the pointers, point to the North Star.

Compasses through the ages

The first explorers had very little to help them find their way around the world. Travelers used simple maps and learned how to find their way, or navigate, using the sun and the stars.

During the day, travelers can always find out where east and west are, because the sun rises in the east and sets in the west. At night, they can use the stars to find out where north and south are. An imaginary line called the *equator* circles the world halfway between the North and South poles. In countries north of the equator, the North Star shows which way is north. A pattern of bright stars called the *Big Dipper* points to Polaris, the North Star. In countries south of the equator, the upright line in a group of stars called the *Southern Cross* points to the south.

This group of stars is called the Southern Cross. Four bright stars make the shape of a cross that points to the south.

Who made the first compass?

No one knows who made the first **magnetic compass**. Legend has it that about 1,000 A.D., a Chinese scientist held up a silk thread attached to the center of a needle and watched the needle point to the south. When he rubbed the needle with a **lodestone**, a hard black magnetic rock, it pointed north.

About 100 years later, sailors began to use magnetic compasses to find their way across the oceans. Until about three or four hundred years ago, most ships carried a piece of lodestone that sailors used to magnetize their compass needles. A long piece of this rock would point north-south if hung by a string.

Modern compasses

Hikers and sailors still use magnetic compasses to tell directions. Small boats use a magnetic compass called a **mariner's** or **maritime compass**. It consists of a ring-shaped magnet attached to a card. The points of the compass are marked on the card. The card and magnet float in a bowl of water mixed with alcohol. The compass always floats horizontally, so that it can work properly even in stormy seas.

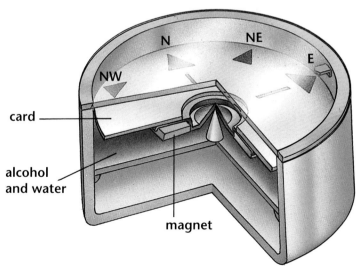

Magnetic compasses don't work near steel or electrical machines. So in addition to radar, or using energy waves to find their way, ships use a special compass called a **gyrocompass.** Gyrocompasses do not use magnetism and can be set to point toward the geographic North Pole.

Can you find north?

You can use your watch to find north whenever the sun is shining. Hold your watch level and point the hour hand at the sun. The north-south line is halfway between the hour hand and the number 12 on your watch. Stand with the place where the sun rises on your right, and point a pencil in the north-south direction. You and the pencil are now pointing to the north.

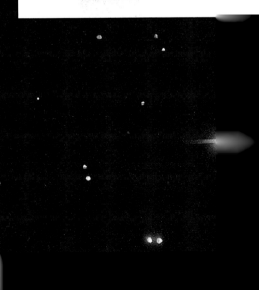

NS line

Electromagnets

An ordinary bar magnet has a magnetic field around it all the time. We call this kind of magnet a permanent magnet. You can also make a magnet by wrapping wire around an iron rod or bolt. When an electric current passes through the wire, the rod works like a magnet. We call this kind of magnet an **electromagnet.** We use electromagnets in many household appliances, such as refrigerators and vacuum cleaners.

Make an electromagnet

You will need:

a plastic or wooden ruler

2 pieces of thin, plastic-coated wire, 20 in. (50 cm) and 40 in. (1 m), with bare ends

adhesive tape

a felt-tip pen

a small compass

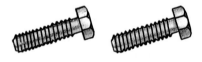

two large iron bolts

a 1.5-volt ("D") battery

a 6-volt battery

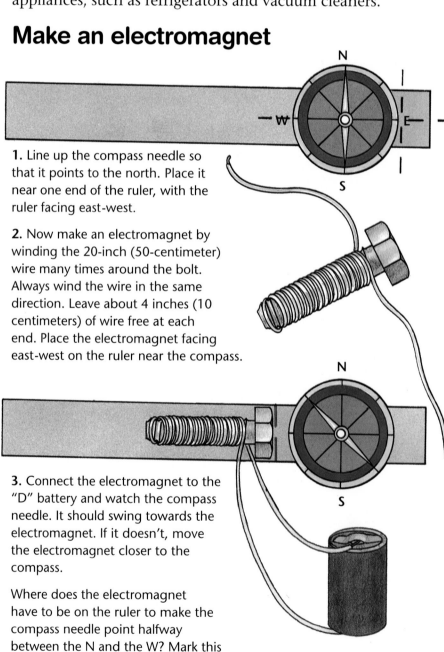

1. Line up the compass needle so that it points to the north. Place it near one end of the ruler, with the ruler facing east-west.

2. Now make an electromagnet by winding the 20-inch (50-centimeter) wire many times around the bolt. Always wind the wire in the same direction. Leave about 4 inches (10 centimeters) of wire free at each end. Place the electromagnet facing east-west on the ruler near the compass.

3. Connect the electromagnet to the "D" battery and watch the compass needle. It should swing towards the electromagnet. If it doesn't, move the electromagnet closer to the compass.

Where does the electromagnet have to be on the ruler to make the compass needle point halfway between the N and the W? Mark this point on the ruler.

4. Now make a second electromagnet with the longer wire, leaving about 6 inches (20 centimeters) of wire free at each end. Disconnect the first electromagnet. Place the second one on the ruler at the mark you made earlier, and connect it to the "D" battery.

What happens to the compass needle? Does it swing around farther than before? Remember, twice as much wire means twice as much resistance. This makes the current half as strong.

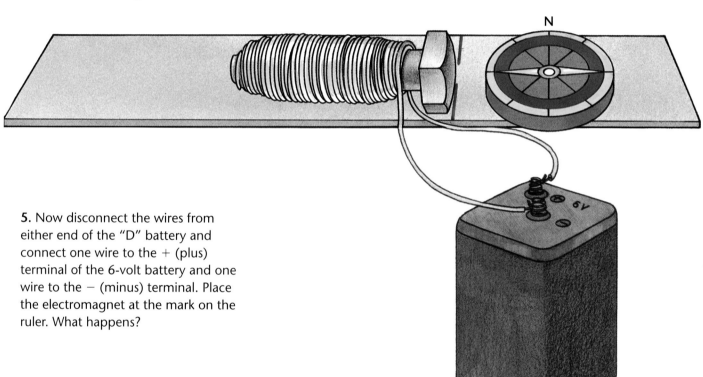

5. Now disconnect the wires from either end of the "D" battery and connect one wire to the + (plus) terminal of the 6-volt battery and one wire to the − (minus) terminal. Place the electromagnet at the mark on the ruler. What happens?

Making an electromagnet stronger

What can you learn from the experiment on this page? The strength of an ordinary bar magnet is permanent and fixed. But we can make the magnetism around an electromagnet weaker or stronger, and we can even turn it off completely.

How can you make an electromagnet stronger? How did you increase the magnetism in the electromagnet?

The electromagnet has become stronger because the 6-volt battery is sending more electric current through it. More electric current makes an electromagnet stronger. The needle moves farther than before.

Magnets in the scrapyard

How many useful things are made of metal? Small items, such as knives and forks, nuts and bolts, and tin cans, are made of metal. So are big objects, such as machines and cars. When we've finished with these things, we shouldn't just throw them away, even if the tin can is crushed, the forks are bent, and the car has broken down and no longer runs. We can send scrap metal to special scrapyards so that it can be used again, or **recycled**, to make new metal products.

magnet

iron and steel scrap

Magnets can move metals

In scrapyards and factories, we use electromagnets attached to giant cranes to move heavy metals from one place to another. The electric current is turned off while the electromagnet is placed near the object that's going to be moved. When the electric current is switched on, the electromagnet attracts the metal object and picks it up. The crane carries the metal to where it's needed, or will be stored. Then the electric current is switched off, so there's no longer any magnetism around the electromagnet. The metal is left behind when the crane moves away. The crane is then ready to pick up another heavy metal object in the scrapyard or factory.

Magnets are used in scrapyards to separate iron and steel scrap from other scrap metals. First, the scrap metal is shredded by being cut into small thin pieces. Then the shredded metal is put onto a moving conveyor belt that has a magnet at one end. The magnet attracts the iron and steel scrap, while the rest of the scrap metal falls into a bin at the end of the conveyor belt.

Magnets are also used at garbage dumps to separate iron and steel from nonmagnetic garbage.

A magnetic roller moves the conveyor belt along. The large magnet separates the iron and steel from other materials.

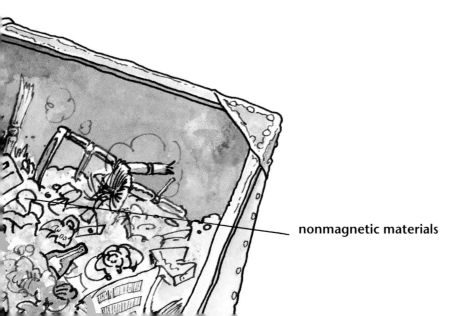

nonmagnetic materials

Electric buzzers

You will need:

two pieces of wood, one about 2 in. (5 cm) × 4 in. (10 cm) and one about 1 in. (2.5 cm) × 2 in. (5 cm)

wood glue

a large nail

a hammer

two pieces of cloth

a thumbtack

two lengths of thin, plastic-coated wire, with bare ends, 80 in. (2 m) and 40 in. (1 m)

a metal nail file with a hole at one end

a 6-volt battery

Did you know that there's an electromagnet inside your telephone? There's also an electromagnet in the meter that measures how much electricity you use in your home. It's electromagnetism that makes the electric buzzer inside a doorbell work. You can make an electromagnetic buzzer and see what makes it buzz!

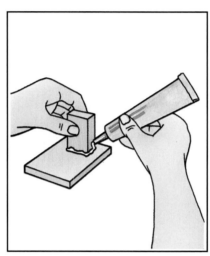

1. Glue the small piece of wood upright near one end of the larger piece of wood. This is the base for your buzzer.

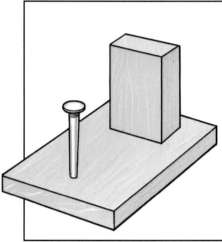

2. Hammer the nail into the other end of the wooden base. The top of the nail should be about $1/16$ inch (1.5 millimeters) below the top of the upright piece of wood.

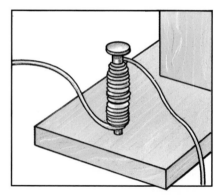

3. Wind the longer wire about 50 times around the nail to make an electromagnet. Always wind the wire in the same direction. Leave about 12 inches (30 centimeters) of wire free at each end.

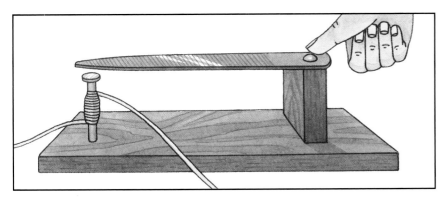

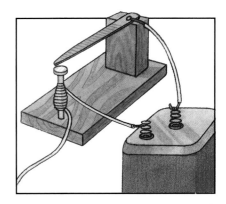

4. Hold the end of the nail file with the small hole above the wooden base. Push a thumbtack through the hole and into the wood. The other end of the blade should be about $1/16$ inch (1.5 millimeters) above the nail.

5. Connect one of the wires from the electromagnet to one terminal of the battery. Connect one end of the shorter wire to the battery and the other end to the thumbtack on the wooden base.

6. Now hold the free wire from the electromagnet and gently touch the top of the nail file with it. The nail file will make a buzzing sound. It won't buzz if it's too near or too far away from the electromagnet.

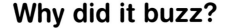

Why did it buzz?

When the bare wire from the electromagnet touches the nail file, an electric current flows through the wire and through the electromagnet. The electric current creates a magnetic field around the electromagnet, and so the metal file is attracted towards the electromagnet.

When the nail file moves towards the electromagnet, breaking contact with the bare wire, the electric current stops flowing. The magnetic field around the electromagnet disappears, and the file springs back and touches the wire. The current flows again and the magnet attracts the nail file again.

As the nail file moves backwards and forwards between the wire and the electromagnet, it makes a buzzing sound.

What is a solenoid?

A **solenoid** is a coil of wire that can be used as an electromagnet. When an electric current flows through it, the electricity creates a magnetic field around the wire. We can make the magnetic field stronger by putting a rod of iron or steel into the solenoid. The magnetic field becomes stronger because the metal rod is magnetized by the solenoid.

Solenoids and magnetic poles

How does a solenoid magnetize an iron rod? The iron rod is made up of a lot of groups of atoms called *domains*. These domains are miniature magnets, but their magnetism has no power because their poles are pointing in different directions. When an iron rod comes into a magnetic field around a solenoid, the domains in the rod all line up and point one way. Then the rod has strong magnetic poles at each end and a magnetic field around it.

When an electric current runs through a solenoid, it has poles just like a bar magnet. One end is a north pole and the other end is a south pole. If you hold an iron or steel rod near a solenoid, the rod becomes magnetized, and the end of the rod that's nearest the north pole of the solenoid becomes a south pole. In the same way, the end of a rod held near the south pole of the solenoid will become a north pole. Unlike poles attract, and so the magnetized rod and the solenoid attract each other.

Like a bar magnet, a solenoid has two poles. The flux lines of the magnetic field link together the north and south poles of the solenoid.

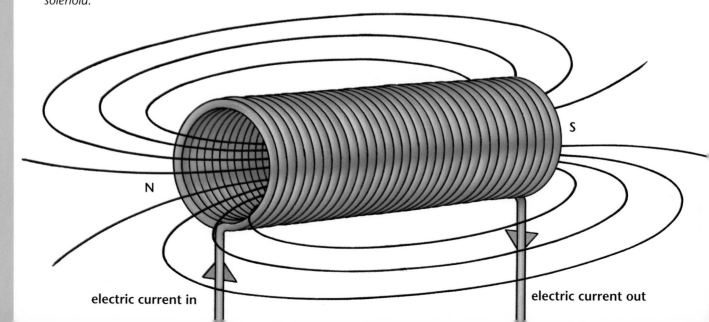

N

S

electric current in

electric current out

You will need:

scissors

40 in. (1 m) of plastic-coated wire, with bare ends

a long steel straight pin

a 6-volt battery

a drinking straw

What can solenoids do?

You can make a solenoid and see for yourself how a steel rod moves inside the coil when the electric current flows.

1. Cut a piece of the drinking straw about 1 inch (2.5 centimeters) long. Wind the wire many times around the short piece of straw to make a solenoid. Always wind the wire in the same direction. Leave about 10 inches (25 centimeters) of wire free at each end.

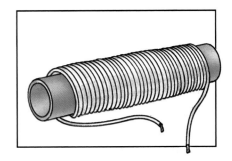

2. Connect one end of the solenoid wire to one terminal of the battery.

3. Stand the pin upright on the table. With the other hand, place the solenoid over the pin. Hold the solenoid upright with the pin inside it.

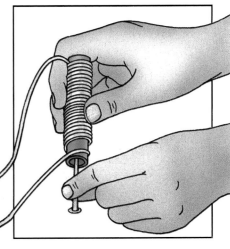

4. Hold the free wire from the solenoid against the free battery terminal and the electric current will flow. **Don't touch the bare end of the wire!** As the current flows, the pin jumps up into the coil. It will stay there until the current is switched off.

5. Now switch the connections to the battery. Does the pin still jump up into the solenoid? Does it matter in which direction the electric current flows through the coil?

Don't take your solenoid apart. You can use it for other experiments in this book.

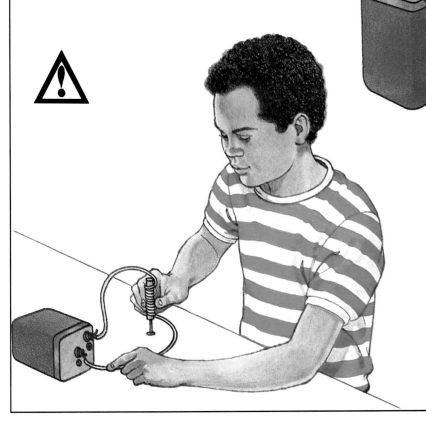

Find out more by looking at pages **98–99**

Solenoids at work

Solenoids can pull iron rods towards them. Can you think of ways in which a solenoid can be useful? Solenoids can work as a kind of switch in electric door locks, in pinball machines, and in electric circuit breakers.

When you press down a switch on an electric door lock, an electric current flows through a solenoid and creates a magnetic field around it. When the current flows, the metal rod in the lock becomes magnetized and is pulled into the coil. This action pulls the bolt back and the door is unlocked.

Solenoids and magnets

If we use a solenoid with a magnet, instead of an ordinary iron rod, the solenoid not only pulls the magnet towards the coil, but also pushes it away. So the magnet moves both backwards and forwards.

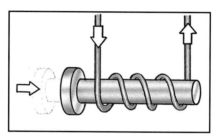

1. When an electric current flows through the coil, the rod becomes magnetized. It is pulled inside the coil.

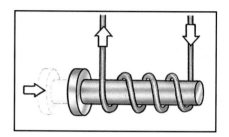

2. The electric current is now reversed and it flows in the opposite direction. The rod is again magnetized and pulled inside the coil.

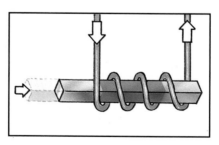

3. The rod is now replaced by a bar magnet. When an electric current flows through the coil, the bar magnet is pulled inside the coil.

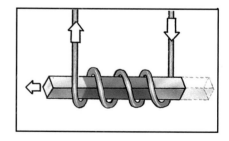

4. What happens when the electric current is reversed? The coil pushes the magnet away. When the current flows in a different direction, the magnet moves in a different direction.

If you hold the magnet still, the coil will move backwards or forwards when the current flows.

Inside a loudspeaker

Loudspeakers can turn electric signals into sounds that we can hear. Inside a loudspeaker there is a solenoid attached to a thin cone, or diaphragm. The solenoid has a powerful magnet inside and outside it. Wires connect the solenoid to a sound system or television. Electric signals from the sound system or TV pass through these wires and the solenoid. The signals change strength and direction, up to 40,000 times a second. As the signals change, varying magnetic forces are created around the solenoid. These forces drive the solenoid alternately toward and away from the magnet in rapid vibrations. As a result, the diaphragm also vibrates, producing sounds we can hear.

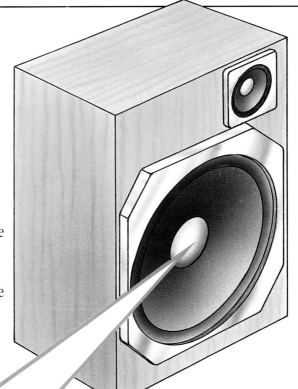

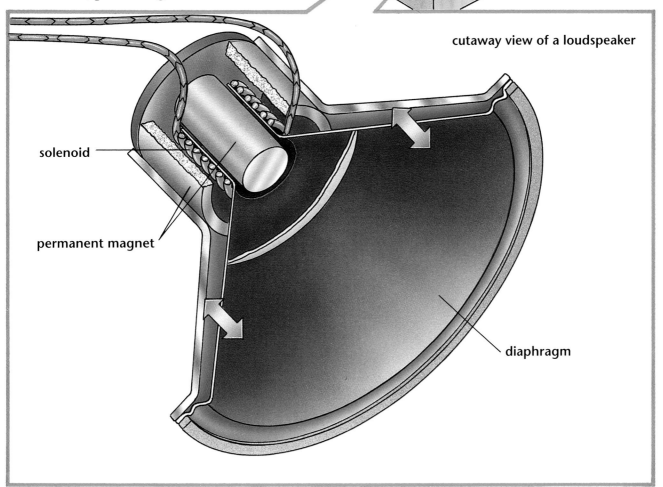

cutaway view of a loudspeaker

solenoid

permanent magnet

diaphragm

Metal detectors

Have you ever hunted for buried treasure? You could just start digging anywhere and hope that you would find something. Or you could use a metal detector to find out exactly where metal objects are buried under the ground. Magnetism makes a metal detector work. Do you know how?

The kind of metal detector that treasure hunters use is often made up of two flat coils of wire fixed to one end of a short pole. At the other end is a handle, and a box containing a battery and electronic sensors.

You can use a metal detector to find buried coins and other metal objects.

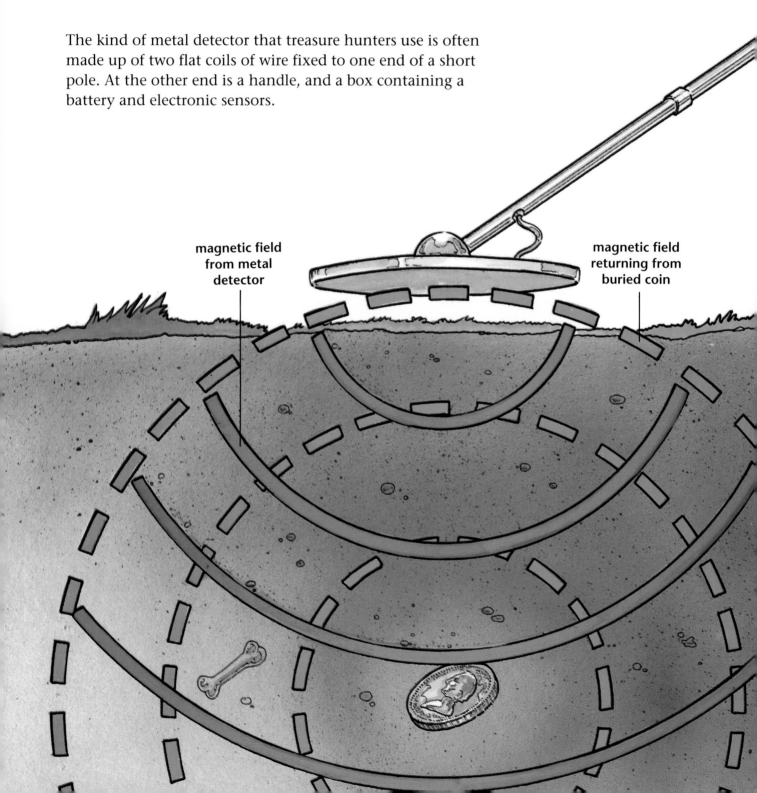

magnetic field from metal detector

magnetic field returning from buried coin

How does a metal detector work?

The magnetic field around one of the coils creates electric currents in any metal object buried in the ground. These currents create a magnetic field around the buried object. The metal detector's other coil receives the magnetic field made by the currents. Electric sensors respond with a beep, light, or message on a display. This tells the treasure hunter that the detector has found a metal object. Other metal detectors have only one coil that sends and detects current.

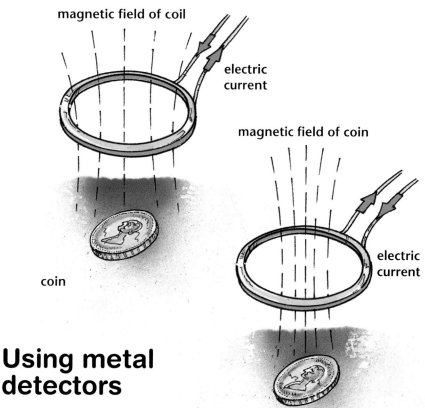

magnetic field of coil

electric current

magnetic field of coin

electric current

coin

Using metal detectors

Can you think of any other uses for a metal detector? There are metal detectors in vending machines to test whether the coins put in the slot are real or fake. There are metal detectors at airports so that security guards can make sure no one takes dangerous weapons, such as guns, onto airplanes. There are also detectors that locate explosive land mines. Metal detectors under the road control some sets of traffic lights, where a major road crosses a minor road. The lights will change to "Go" for the minor road only when a car comes along. Magnetism makes all these different kinds of metal detectors work.

Find out more by looking at pages **92–93**

Magnets and electric motors

Electric motors run lots of everyday machines, such as hairdryers and vacuum cleaners. How does a motor work? Magnetism and electric current work together to cause a coil inside the motor to rotate.

Direct and alternating current

There are two kinds of electric current—**direct current** (DC) and **alternating current** (AC). Direct current always flows in the same direction through an electric circuit. Alternating current changes direction many times every second. So there are also two main types of electric motors—DC motors and AC motors. DC motors usually run from battery power. Here is a cutaway view of a DC motor.

The **fixed electromagnet,** or field magnet, of this DC motor creates a magnetic field with north and south poles. Magnetism and electric current together run the motor.

The **commutator** consists of two semicircular rings. This part of the motor changes the direction of the electric current to keep the armature turning.

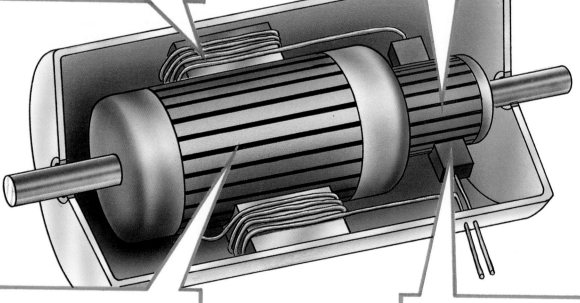

The **rotating coil,** or armature, becomes an electromagnet when current passes through. The armature turns as its poles are attracted and then repelled by the fixed magnet's poles.

Two **brushes** in the motor transmit current. One brush carries the current from the battery. The second brush, on the other side of the commutator, sends current back to the battery.

DC and AC motors

We use DC motors to drive electric trains. These trains need the most power when they accelerate from a standing position. DC motors can develop full power at different speeds, even developing great power when turning very slowly. The electric current is carried to the train from the rails below, or from overhead wires.

We use AC motors in kitchen appliances, vacuum cleaners, and other machines that run at a steady speed. AC motors can be just as powerful as DC motors, but it's more difficult to change the speed of an AC motor. The electricity sent to our homes from power stations is alternating current, and so these domestic appliances use the electricity directly, without having to convert it.

*The French TGV (train à grand vitesse or high-speed train) is the world's fastest electric train. The latest TGV's can reach speeds of about 185 miles (300 kilometers) per hour. Alternating current (AC) is carried to the train through overhead wires. Devices called **rectifiers** inside the locomotive change the AC to direct current (DC).*

Find out more by looking at pages **104–105**

Inside a generator

In the early 1800's, a Danish scientist named Hans Oersted was the first person to notice that there was a link between magnetism and electricity. In 1831, an English scientist named Michael Faraday made the first machine that used magnetism to make electric currents. This machine was called a **dynamo**, or **generator.**

When a wire is moving within a magnetic field, an electric current flows in the wire. Inside a simple generator, a mechanical engine rotates a coil of wire in the magnetic field between two magnetic poles. As the coil turns, an electric current flows in the wire.

How does the electric current travel?

How does the electricity in the coil travel to where it will be used? The two wire ends of the coil are connected to two rings, called *slip rings*. These slip rings rotate at the same time as the coil. Two fixed pieces of carbon, called *brushes*, rest against the slip rings. Thus the electricity flows from the coil, to the slip rings, through the brushes, and into wires that carry the current to wherever it is needed.

A simple generator consists of a coil of wire that rotates between the two poles of a magnet. As the coil rotates, an electric current flows in the coil. The current is carried from the generator through the brushes, which press against the slip rings.

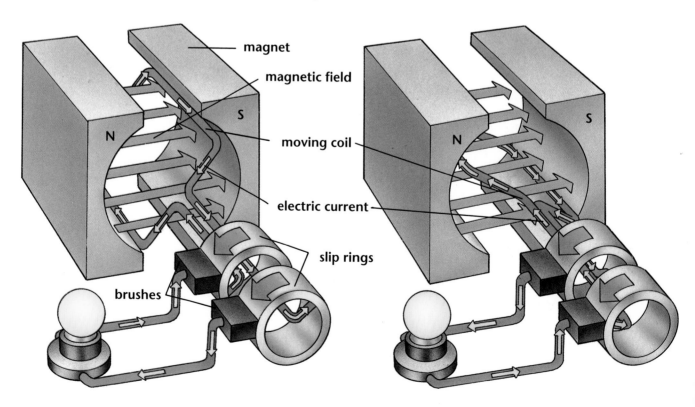

magnet

magnetic field

moving coil

electric current

slip rings

brushes

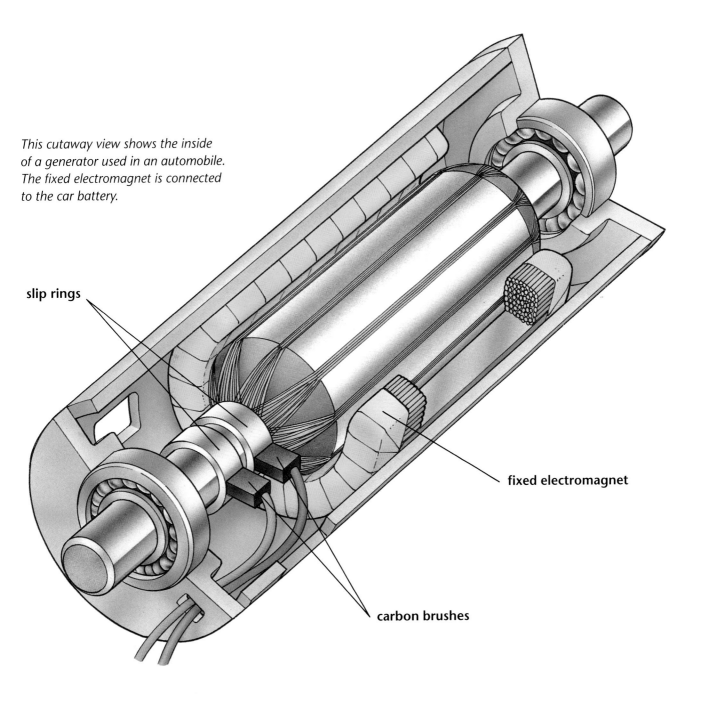

This cutaway view shows the inside of a generator used in an automobile. The fixed electromagnet is connected to the car battery.

slip rings

fixed electromagnet

carbon brushes

Different kinds of generators

Generators can be small enough to hold in your hand, or bigger than a house. Some kinds of generators produce direct current electricity, and other kinds of generators produce alternating current electricity.

Find out more by looking at pages **110–111**

Floating magnets

Have you ever heard of the Indian rope trick? Magicians in India who perform this famous conjuring trick make a rope appear to stand upright from the ground with nothing holding it up.

Other magicians can make objects, and even people, seem to float in the air with nothing holding them up. This is called **levitation**. We can use magnets to make things **levitate**, or float in the air. Try it yourself with a simple experiment.

Magnetic magic

You will need:

cotton thread

a paper clip

masking tape

a sheet of paper

a strong magnet

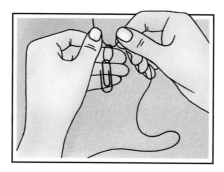

1. Tie one end of the cotton thread to a paper clip.

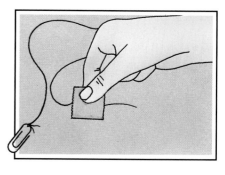

2. Tape the other end of the thread to the top of a table, using masking tape.

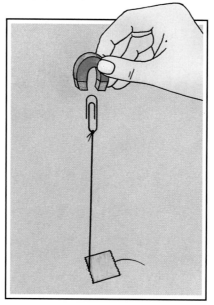

3. Can you make the thread stand up without letting the magnet touch the paper clip?

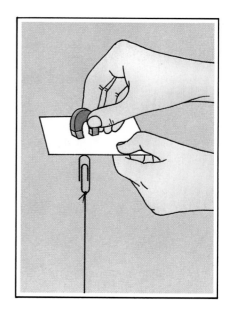

4. Pass a sheet of paper between the magnet and the paper clip to show that they are not touching.

You will need:

scissors

stiff plain paper, about
8 in. (20 cm) × 2 in. (5 cm)

masking tape

two strong bar magnets

Magnetic levitation

The paper clip appeared to float in the air because it was attracted to the magnet. You can also make things levitate when two magnets repel each other.

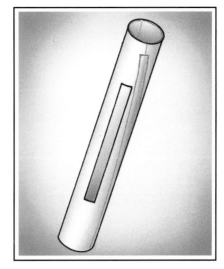

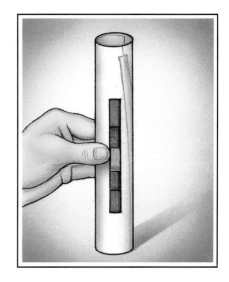

1. Cut a long, thin slot lengthwise in the center of the paper. The slot should be about 5 inches (12.75 centimeters) long and ¹/₈ inch (3.25 millimeters) wide. Then roll the paper into a tube shape and put masking tape along the long edge.

2. Place the two magnets inside the tube with the north poles of both magnets facing each other. What do you see through the slot? How are the poles reacting?

What happens when the two south poles are facing each other?

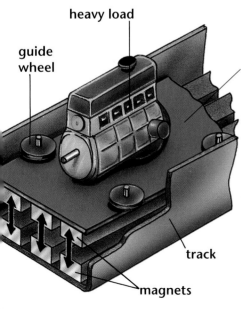

heavy load

guide wheel

moving platform

track

magnets

Scientists have used this idea of magnetic levitation to make a special magnetic track. This track can be used instead of a conveyor belt to help move heavy loads.

Magnets are attached to the bottom of a U-shaped track. These magnets repel other magnets that are fixed under a moving platform. A heavy load, such as a car engine, is then placed on the platform. Small wheels on the platform prevent the load from moving sideways and keep the magnets facing each other. If electromagnets are used, they can be switched on and off to make the load move along.

Find out more by looking
at pages **108–109**

Magnetic trains

Can you imagine trains that move along floating in the air? The **magnetic levitation train**, known as a **maglev train**, is already in service in Birmingham, England and Berlin, Germany. Another type of magnetic train is still being perfected. It is a high-speed passenger train known as a **magnetic levitation vehicle, MLV**. These trains are quieter than ordinary trains and are the fastest trains ever made, but they are more expensive to build because they need a special kind of track known as a **guideway.**

There are two types of maglev trains—*electrodynamic* and *electromagnetic*. Electrodynamic maglevs use magnetic repulsion (pushing away) to make the train float above the guideway. The magnetic force is so strong that it can raise and hold a train full of passengers 4 inches (10 centimeters) above the guideway.

Electromagnetic maglevs use magnetic attraction. When an electric current flows through the magnets under the guideway, they are attracted upward to steel rails on the guideway.

The magnetic levitation, or maglev train, floats in the air. Magnets on the underside of the train and on the guide rails below create a powerful magnetic force that holds the train above the rails and drives it forward.

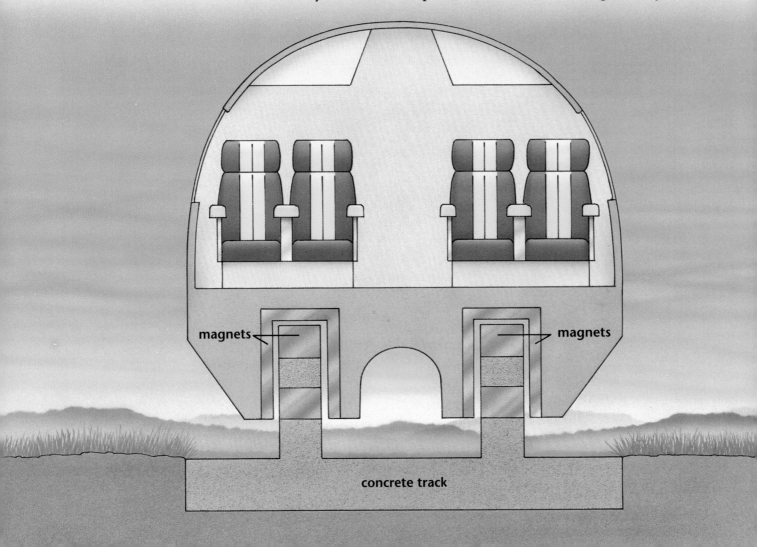

magnets

magnets

concrete track

How do magnetic trains work?

Magnetic trains are powered by a type of motor called a **linear electric motor.** The word *linear* means "in a line." The linear motor works in the same way as any other electric motor, but it moves in a straight line instead of turning in a circular rotation. The track is a long, straight electromagnet. When an electric current flows through this electromagnet, the train is pushed along the track in the same way that an ordinary motor pushes a coil of wire around and around. Changing the electric current can make a magnetic train start, stop or change its speed.

Magnetic trains may one day travel as fast as 300 miles (480 kilometers) per hour. Ordinary trains cannot go so fast because the friction, or rubbing, of their wheels on the track makes them lose speed.

This maglev railcar travels along an elevated track between the railway station and international airport in Birmingham, England.

112

Find out more by looking at pages **110–111**

Superconductors

An electric current can flow through ordinary metal wires, known as **conductors**, made from copper or aluminum. These wires conduct the electric current, which is a flow of electrical energy. In most conductors, moving electrons are always colliding with atoms and losing energy. This lost energy is turned into heat energy. Scientists say that the wire has a **resistance** to the electric current.

When metal wires are cooled down to a very low temperature, the electrons in the metal move around without losing energy. This loss of resistance means that the current can flow more easily through the wire. Metals in this state are called **superconductors.** An electric current flows easily through a superconductor, and none of the electrical energy is turned into heat energy.

How can we use superconductors?

Scientists are finding ways to use superconducting materials. They are testing superconducting switching devices for computers. Superconducting materials may also allow medical equipment to detect very small magnetic fields, which would help doctors diagnose disease in their patients. Superconductivity may also help in making smaller and more efficient electric motors and generators.

The vibrating electrons in the metal wire make it difficult for the current to flow. Some of the electrical energy turns into heat energy and warms up the wire.

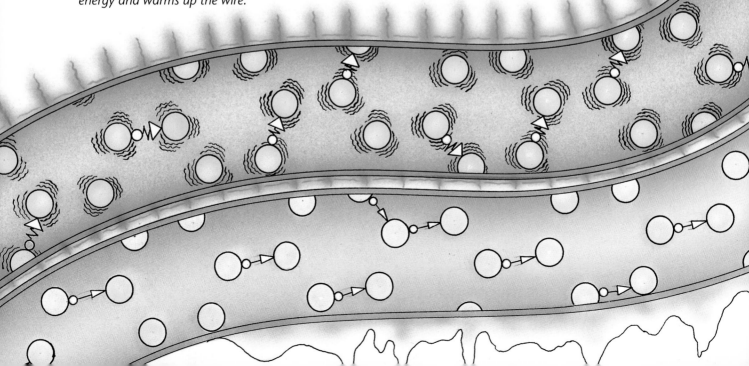

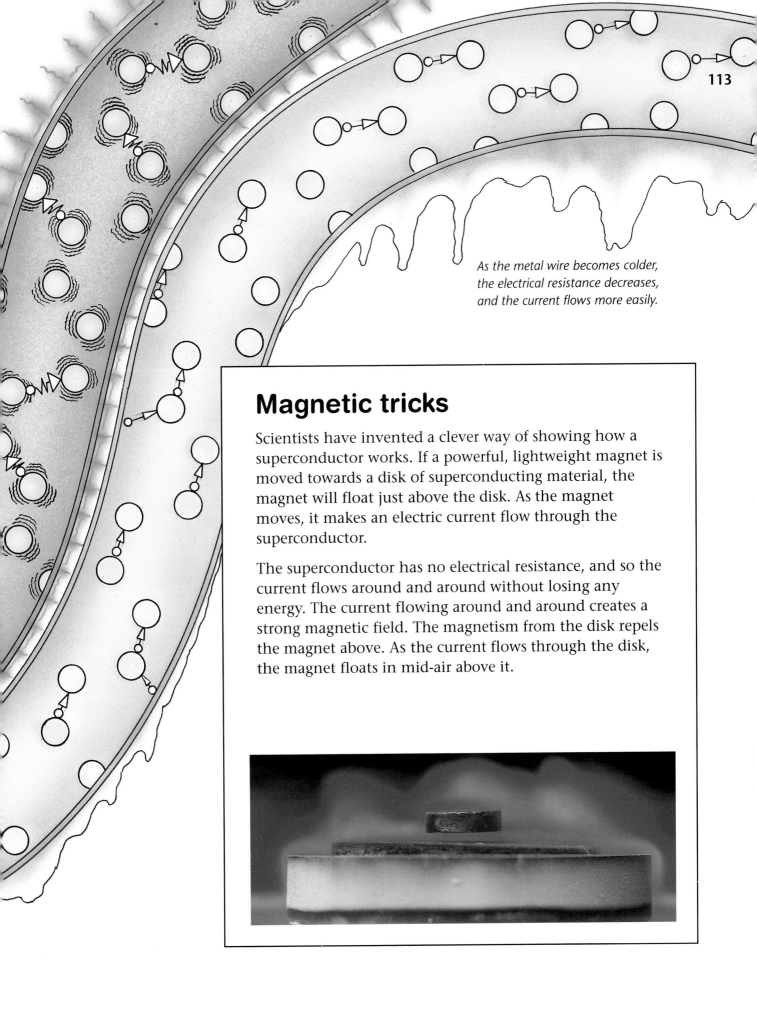

As the metal wire becomes colder, the electrical resistance decreases, and the current flows more easily.

Magnetic tricks

Scientists have invented a clever way of showing how a superconductor works. If a powerful, lightweight magnet is moved towards a disk of superconducting material, the magnet will float just above the disk. As the magnet moves, it makes an electric current flow through the superconductor.

The superconductor has no electrical resistance, and so the current flows around and around without losing any energy. The current flowing around and around creates a strong magnetic field. The magnetism from the disk repels the magnet above. As the current flows through the disk, the magnet floats in mid-air above it.

Find out more by looking at pages **96–97**

Place your electric buzzer beside an AM radio. Switch on the radio and then touch the bare wire to the metal file above the nail. You should hear a buzzing and crackling sound coming from your radio.

Electromagnetic radiation

Do you remember the electric buzzer you made earlier? Place the buzzer beside an AM radio that you have switched on. When you connect the buzzer, a buzzing and crackling noise comes from the radio's loudspeaker. Your buzzer is sending out energy that the radio then picks up. This travels through the space between your buzzer and your radio.

Your buzzer worked by switching the electric current on and off very quickly. When the current was on, a magnetic field developed around the wires in the circuit. When the current was off, the magnetic field collapsed. When this happened, a form of energy called **electromagnetic radiation** traveled out from the wires. It was this energy that caused the crackling.

As the electromagnetic radiation moves outward from its source, its energy constantly changes from strong to weak and back again. The changing energy sets up a pattern that scientists call **waves.**

What is wavelength?

Electromagnetic waves travel through space in a straight line, and their electric and magnetic fields move back and forth at right angles to each other and at a right angle to the energy flow. Scientists can determine the distance between two points where the electric and magnetic fields repeat—for example, from a point of maximum field strength in a certain direction to the next point of maximum field strength in the same direction. This distance is called the **wavelength** of the electromagnetic radiation and is usually measured in meters or fractions of meters.

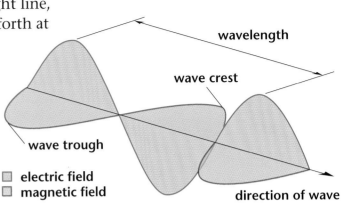

What is frequency?

Count how often a ball bounces against a wall and back in one minute. You are measuring how often, or how frequently, the ball bounces during a certain time. Scientists measure electromagnetic radiation by counting the number of times the electric field and the magnetic field change from a maximum in one direction, to zero, to a maximum in the opposite direction, back to zero, and back to a maximum in the original direction. This change is called one complete cycle of the wave. The number of complete cycles in one second is called the **frequency.** We measure frequency in units called **hertz,** or **Hz.**

The frequency of the red wave is lower than the frequency of the blue wave. This is because the wavelength of the red wave is longer.

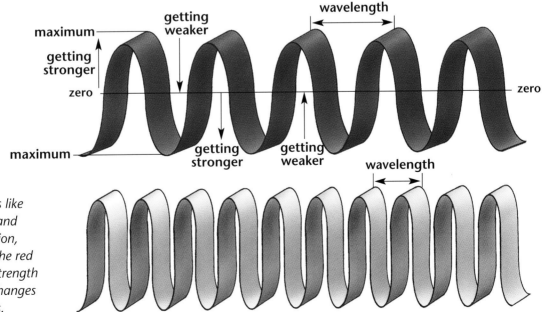

Scientists draw pictures like this to help us understand electromagnetic radiation, such as radio waves. The red wave shows how the strength of the magnetic field changes as a radio wave travels.

Find out more by looking at pages **114–115**

The electromagnetic spectrum

Electromagnetic radiation travels out in every direction from the point, or source, where it is generated. This radiation travels out at an enormous speed—186,282 miles (299,792 kilometers) per second in a vacuum. In other words, electromagnetic radiation would take more than one second to reach the moon, which is about 239,000 miles (384,500 kilometers) away from Earth.

The frequency of electromagnetic radiation can be lower than a few thousand hertz. Or it may be higher than billions of hertz. Scientists call the range of different frequencies the **electromagnetic spectrum.** At one end of the electromagnetic spectrum are gamma rays, which have the highest frequencies. At the other end of the spectrum are radio waves, which have the lowest frequencies. In between are X rays, ultraviolet waves, visible light, infrared radiation, and microwaves.

Scientists have developed a variety of appliances, devices, and instruments that use electromagnetic radiation to help us in our daily life. These appliances include X-ray machines, cameras, microwave ovens, solar-powered calculators, security alarms, televisions, and radios.

Gamma rays are given off by radioactive materials. They are detected by a machine called a Geiger counter. Gamma rays can pass through thick pieces of most kinds of metal.

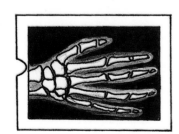

X rays have very high energy and so pass easily through many different materials. X rays are used to make X-ray photographs of the bones inside our bodies.

High-frequency ultraviolet light helps infants born with jaundice, a liver disorder.

Solar-powered calculators use energy from visible light to generate electricity. This is called the **photoelectric effect.**

The whole range of electromagnetic radiation frequencies is called the electromagnetic spectrum. It includes radio waves, infrared and ultraviolet waves, and X rays.

Infrared lamps are used in restaurants to keep food hot before being served. The infrared rays produce heat when they strike the food.

Microwave dishes can beam signals accurately from one place to another. These dishes sometimes beam telephone conversations between exchanges.

Television stations transmit high frequency radio waves. Many of these waves are transmitted via satellites in the sky.

This remote control sends invisible signals of infrared radiation to a television to change the channel, the brightness, or the sound.

Inside a microwave oven, microwave energy causes the water molecules in the food to vibrate quickly, and so the food cooks.

Radio stations transmit electromagnetic waves that are picked up by radio receivers. Some waves are transmitted across the world.

Alternating current: *Electric current* that changes direction many times every second.

Ampere: Unit for measuring the flow of an *electric current.*

Atmosphere: Air surrounding Earth.

Atom: Smallest part of a substance. An atom contains a mass of *protons* and *neutrons* in a center called a *nucleus,* which is surrounded by *electrons.* All things on Earth are made of atoms.

Circuit breaker: Switch that automatically interrupts an *electric circuit* when the current gets too strong.

Compound eye: Eye made up of many tiny lenses set at different angles. Some insects have compound eyes.

Concave: Shaped like the inside of a dish; rounded inward.

Conductor: Material that allows an *electric current* to flow through it.

Convex: Shaped in an outward curve.

Direct current: *Electric current* that flows in only one direction.

Electric circuit: Path followed by an *electric current.*

Electric current: Movement of electric charges.

Electromagnet: Coil of wire around an iron bar, that acts as a magnet when an *electric current* passes through the wire.

Electromagnetic energy: Energy consisting of two sorts of energy—electrical and magnetic.

Electromagnetic radiation: Another word for *radiant energy.*

Electromagnetic spectrum: All the forms of radiant energy, which are measured by their frequency and wavelength. The electromagnetic spectrum ranges from gamma rays, which have the shortest wavelength, to X rays, ultraviolet radiation, visible light, infrared radiation, and radio waves, which have the longest wavelength.

Electromagnetic wave: Related patterns of electric and magnetic energy. They are made by back-and-forth movement of electric charges.

Electron: Tiny particle that carries a negative electrical charge. Every atom normally has one or more electrons around its center, or *nucleus.* The movement of many electrons is an *electric current.*

Endoscope: Instrument that uses *optical fibers* to look inside someone's body.

Fiber optics: Method of using *optical fibers* to carry images and messages. Fiber optics is used in medicine and communications.

Field of vision: Everything that can be seen when looking straight ahead and to the sides.

Filament: Very thin thread or threadlike part or object. The wire that gives off light in a light bulb is a filament.

Flux lines: Imaginary lines that pass from one magnet to the other, and from a magnet's north pole to its south pole.

Frequency: Number of times something occurs.

Fuse: Electrical safety device that has a piece of metal that melts when the current becomes too strong. When this occurs, the circuit is interrupted and the flow of electricity is turned off, preventing a fire.

Geothermal energy: Energy trapped in the hot rocks below Earth's surface.

Hologram: Special photograph that appears as a three-dimensional picture. It is made using laser light. Three-dimensional pictures show an object in its three dimensions—its depth, its length, and its width.

Infrared rays: Rays that cannot be seen, but are felt as heat. Infrared rays help make us feel warm when we stand in the sunshine.

Insulator: Material that doesn't let an electric current flow through it.

Invisible spectrum: *Radiant energy* that cannot be seen.

Ion: An atom or group of atoms that has an electric charge.

Laser: Device that makes light travel in a very narrow beam.

Light: A form of energy that can travel freely through space.

Light, artificial: Source of light that doesn't occur naturally, but is made by people.

Light, fluorescent: Special kind of light that changes more of the electrical energy it uses into light and less into heat.

Light, natural: Source of light not created by people.

Light, white: Light that has no color, but is made up of different colors. White light is a mixture of all the colors of the rainbow, including red, orange, yellow, green, blue, and violet.

Magnetic field: Space surrounding a magnet.

Magnetism: Invisible force that can make some things move toward each other, move away from each other, or stay in one place.

Melanin: Substance produced by the skin that protects it from sunburn caused by ultraviolet rays.

Multimeter: A device used to measure electric current, voltage, and resistance.

Nucleus: Middle part of an *atom*. The nucleus contains *neutrons* and *protons* and can produce energy.

Optical fiber: Thread of glass or plastic.

Ozone: Layer of gas high up in the atmosphere that prevents most of the *ultraviolet* rays from reaching Earth.

Periscope: Tube containing several lenses and mirrors, with which it is possible to see from the bottom of the tube whatever can be seen at the top.

Photon: The particle that makes up light and all other forms of electromagnetic radiation.

Pole: Either end of a magnet or flashlight battery.

Primary color of light: The three colors in the color spectrum—red, green, and blue—that, when combined together in nearly equal amounts, make white light. Any other color of light can be made by mixing two or three primary colors of light.

Prism: A specially shaped transparent block of glass or plastic that breaks up *white light* into a rainbowlike band of color called the *visible spectrum.*

Radiant energy: All the forms of energy that together make up the *electromagnetic spectrum.* The sun gives off all forms of radiant energy. The various types of radiant energy have different wavelengths and frequencies. Radiant energy is also called *electromagnetic radiation.*

Reflecting telescope: A telescope that uses bowl-shaped mirrors instead of lenses to form an image of a star or other heavenly body. The mirrors reflect the light waves to a focus.

Reflection: Something that is turned back from a surface.

Refracting telescope: Simple telescope made up of two lenses—one at either end of a narrow tube. The large lens at the front bends the light that enters it. It produces an image at the other end that is viewed through a second lens.

Refraction: Change in the direction in which light waves travel when they pass from one kind of matter into another.

Short circuit: What results when two bare wires touch each other, allowing an electric current to pass directly from one wire to the other.

Solar energy: Energy from the sun.

Solenoid: Coil of wire can be used as an *electromagnet.*

Transformer: Instrument that can make an *electric current* smaller or larger.

Tungsten: Thin coil of metal that gives off light and gets very hot when an electric current passes through it.

Visible spectrum: The only part of all the different kinds of radiant energy that we can see. This part is the rainbowlike band of colors we call *light.*

Volt: A unit that measures *electromotive force,* the "push" and "pull" that makes electrons flow around an electric circuit.

Wavelength: Distance between the top of one wave and the top of the next wave.

White light: A mixture of all the colors in the *visible spectrum.*

R

rabbit, 46
radiant energy, 20
radio, *79*
radio station, *117*
radio wave, *115,* 116–117
railroad, see **train**
rainbow, 14–15, *16*
rattlesnake, 22
rechargeable battery, 55
rectifier, *105*
recycling, 94
red, 16–17, 25, *39, 115*
reflecting telescope, 31
reflection, 12–13, 18–19, 28–29
refracting telescope, 30
refraction, 14–15, 26–27, 32, 39
remote control, *117*
repulsion, see **attraction and repulsion**
resistance, 64, 112–113
rotating coil, *104*
rubber, 59

S

scanner, 41
scrapyard, 94
short circuit, *67*
shutter, camera, 34
silver, 59
simple eye, 47
skin, melanin in, 21
sky, color of, 38–39
slip ring, 106–107
socket, electric, 58
solar energy, 74–75
solar-powered calculator, *116*
solenoid, 98–101

Southern Cross, 90
south magnetic pole (Earth), 86
south pole, of magnet, 81, 82, 96
South Pole (Earth), 86
spectrum, 16
   electromagnetic, 20, 116–117
   invisible, 20
   visible, 20
speed of light, 36–37
step-down transformer, 72
step-up transformer, 72
stereoscopic vision, 46
stimulated emission, 40
submarine, 29
sun
   as light source, 8, 14
   Earth's magnetism and, 87
   magnetic field of, *85*
   sky color and rays from, 38–39
sunburn, 21
sunflower, 18
sunrise, 39
sunset, 38–39
superconductor, 112–113
surgery, 41
switch, electric, 66, 100

T

Taj Mahal, *28*
telephone, 45
telephone pole, *50*
telescope, 30–31
television set, 22
television station, *117*
terminal, battery, 53
TGV train, *105*
thermogram, 23

train, *79, 105,* 110–111
transformer, 72–73
translucent plastic, 19
tungsten, 64
Tunisia, *27*
turbine, 70–71

U

ultraviolet rays, 20–21, 47, 116–117

V

VCR, , see **videocassette recorder**
videocassette recorder, 22
viewfinder, camera, 34
violet, 16, 25, *39*
vision, 46–47
vitamin D, 9, 21
volcano, 38
Volta, Alessandro, 60
volt and voltage, 60–61, 72

W

waterwheel, 74
wave
   electromagnetic, 20, 114–117
   light, 12, 16
wavelength, 16, 115
wax, *10*
welding, *63*
white, 14–15, *17,* 18, *19,* 25
windmill, 74–75
wire, electrical, 58–59, 64, 112
wood, burning of, 74

X

X rays, 116–117

Y

yellow, *17*, 18, *19*

Z

zinc-carbon battery, 54

Acknowledgements

The publishers of **World Book's** *Young Scientist* acknowledge the following photographers, publishers, agencies, and corporations for photographs used in this volume.

Cover	© PhotoDisc, Inc.; © A. J. Verkaik, The Stock Market
2/3	© A. J. Verkaik, The Stock Market
8/9	© A. J. Verkaik, ZEFA Picture Library; © Adam Hart-Davis, Science Photo Library
10/11	© Robert Harding Picture Library; © ZEFA Picture Library; © John Helseltine, Science Photo Library
12–15	© ZEFA Picture Library
16/17	© G. G. Hunter, Bruce Coleman Collection; WORLD BOOK photo by Arnold Ryan Chalfant and Associates
18/19	© Hutchison Library
20/21	© Philippe Plailly, Science Photo Library; NASA from Science Photo Library
22/23	NASA from Science Photo Library; © R. Clark and M. R. Goff, Science Photo Library
26/27	© Havlicek, ZEFA Picture Library
28/29	© ZEFA Picture Library
30/31	© Lori Stiles, University of Arizona; © David Nunuk/SPL from Photo Researchers
36/37	© Bill Wood, Bruce Coleman Collection
38/39	© Armstrong, ZEFA Picture Library
40/41	© Sam C. Pierson, Jr., Photo Researchers; © L. Mulvehill, The Image Works
42/43	© Philippe Plailly, Science Photo Library; © L. S. Stepanowicz, Visuals Unlimited
44/45	© Petit Format, Nestlé from Science Photo Library; © ZEFA Picture Library
46/47	© Armstrong, ZEFA Picture Library; © J. Burgess, Science Photo Library
48–51	© Spectrum Colour Library
54/55	© David R. Frazier
56/57	© ZEFA Picture Library
58/59	© J. Beecham, Spectrum Colour Library
62/63	© Dick Blume, The Image Works
64/65	© ZEFA Picture Library
68/69	© Spencer Grant, PhotoEdit
74/75	© Nicholas Devore, Bruce Coleman Collection
80–85	© ZEFA Picture Library
104/105	© R. Stott, The Image Works
110/111	© Martin Bond, Science Photo Library
112/113	© David Parker, Science Photo Library

Illustrated by

Martin Aitchinson
Nigel Alexander
Hemesh Alles
Martyn Andrews
Sue Barclay
Richard Berridge
John Booth
Lou Bory
Maggie Brand
Stephen Brayfield
Bristol Illustrators
Colin Brown
Estelle Carol
David Cook
Marie DeJohn
Richard Deverell
Farley, White and Veal
Sheila Galbraith
Peter Geissler
Jeremy Gower
Kathie Kelleher
Stuart Lafford

John Lobban
Louise Martin
Annabel Milne
Yoshi Miyake
Donald Moss
Eileen Mueller Neill
Teresa O'Brien
Paul Perreault
Roberta Polfus
Jeremy Pyke
Trevor Ridley
Barry Rowe
Don Simpson
Gary Slater
Lawrie Taylor
Gwen Tourret
Pat Tourret
Peter Visscher
David Webb
Gerald Whitcomb
Matthew White
Lynne Willey